W9-CHL-961

MANAGING ANXIETY
and
STRESS

James Archer, Jr.
Director, University Counseling Center
Associate Professor, Counselor Education
University of Florida
Gainesville, Florida

Accelerated Development Inc.
3400 Kilgore Avenue
Muncie, Indiana 47304
Tel. (317) 284-7511

Library of Congress Catalog Card Number: 81-68413

International Standard Book Number: 0-915202-32-8

© Copyright 1982 by Accelerated Development Inc.
Second Printing January 1985

All rights reserved. No part of this book may be reproduced or transmitted in any form or by any means, electronic or mechanical, including photocopying, recording or by any informational storage and retrieval system, without permission in writing from Accelerated Development Inc.

Coordinator: Cindy Lyons

Editor: Gwen Miller

Graphic Artist: Barbara Sans

Printed in the United States of America

For additional copies order from

Accelerated Development Inc.
3400 Kilgore Avenue
Muncie, Indiana 47304
Tel. (317) 284-7511

PREFACE

My two year old son recently developed a new way to manage his fear and anxiety. Whenever he sees me getting out the power lawnmower he exclaims, "Lawnmower scare Brian," and then scurries away to the opposite end of the yard. Although I have tried to teach him how to "manage" his anxiety, he still prefers to run away in panic every time he sees or hears the lawnmower.

This inability to teach my son to manage this anxiety, in addition to being a useful humbling experience, has served to remind me how difficult it can be to teach anxiety management. In writing this book I have tried to keep this difficulty and the complexity of the subject clearly in mind. At times however in order to include a number of different techniques and to emphasize application I have had to oversimplify. Many of the techniques and approaches may tend to sound easier to use than they are in reality. Every approach covered requires work and effort on the part of the learner.

One strong point of the "cookbook" approach used in this book is the variety of possibilities offered. You will not necessarily find every approach useful, but chances are great that you will find one or two methods that work well for you. It is important to keep a kind of experimental perspective as you go through the different chapters. Do not feel that every approach must work for you. Remember also that these different approaches are not mutually exclusive. In fact, they fit together quite well, and in many ways can help you develop a holistic approach to anxiety management by which you examine your anxiety process from many different angles.

iii

This book is divided into four parts. Part I focuses on nature and impact of anxiety and on anxiety awareness. Part II covers anxiety management approaches that deal primarily with physical health and relaxation, and Part III presents cognitive (thoughts and beliefs) approaches. Part IV deals with life style issues and anxiety management.

The anxiety management program presented will be useful to people working individually or in groups such as classes, workshops, seminars, and other group situations. If you are planning to work alone, periodically discuss with friends some of the issues raised. You can learn much about how to manage anxiety just by finding out how a variety of other people cope with various life stressors.

In general I have followed the same format for each chapter. First, a description of the method being covered is presented. Next is a discussion of how to apply the method interlaced with examples and specific instructions. This phase is followed by a summary and a number of self-assessment/discussion questions. These questions are designed to test your understanding of the chapter and to encourage personal awareness and application. In most chapters a number of activities also are suggested to facilitate personal learning and application. References for each chapter are provided also.

Teachers, counselors, and other course or workshop leaders who are using this book can, of course, adapt it for their own use. I do believe that discussion and experience with the different methods is crucial. Because some of the questions are rather personal, leaders will have to be sensitive to individuals who may be threatened by the self-disclosure involved. I have used these materials with a variety of people, individually and in groups, and have seldom encountered much reluctance; however, it is absolutely essential that participants not be forced to reveal more personal material than they are comfortable in doing.

This material can best be used if participants are given time to try new approaches and discuss their reactions. Weekly sessions with homework of trying the method under consideration work well. Also, practicing each approach in the group or workshop setting helps encourage personal application later. These activities are designed to encourage this application.

I am greatly indebted to the originators of many of the approaches that I have used in this book. In many instances my contribution has been an attempt to make a particular method easier to use and understand. I have tried to maintain the integrity of each approach by including some of the original author's own descriptions. My understanding of how anxiety can be managed with different approaches comes from my experiences with hundreds of different students and clients. I am grateful to all these people for their willingness to trust me and their courage in attempting to confront and overcome negative forms of anxiety. I also am grateful to colleagues and to my wife and family who often have helped me better understand and manage my own anxiety.

A number of typists (Susan Schrank, Arlene Kelley, Jeanette Stant, Karen Hutton, and Charlette Dixon) have worked on this manuscript. I am indebted to them not only for their fine clerical skills, but also for their comments and words of encouragement. My wife, Karen, also has spent many hours helping me clarify my writing and my ideas.

CONTENTS

LIST OF TABLES

LIST OF FIGURES

MANAGING ANXIETY and STRESS

PART I

AWARENESS

PART I

AWARENESS

Part I basically is an introduction to the concept of anxietymanagement. It includes some basic definitions, as well as information on anxiety awareness.

Chapter 1 includes a discussion of the nature of stress and anxiety, presentation of a definition, some different perspectives on anxiety, and a list of some of the negative effects of excessive stress and anxiety.

Chapter 2 contains a triad approach to managing anxiety which includes a brief discussion of anxiety management as related to body, mind, and life style. The process of anxiety management in each of these three areas is discussed and importance of interactions between these three areas is stressed.

In Chapter 3 you will begin to examine your own anxiety process. The purpose of this chapter is to teach you how to increase your awareness of anxiety in a variety of ways. You will be asked to consider your anxiety from the following perspectives: (1) stressful situations, (2) physiological responses, (3) thoughts and fantasies, (4) related feelings, (5) related behavior, (6) blocked and denied anxiety, and (7) delayed reactions.

Chapter 1

NATURE OF ANXIETY

Anxiety is a natural human reaction. Each person has experienced the quickness of breath and the tenseness of muscle that accompanies anxiety. A person cannot grow or develop unless he/she experiences the anxiety that comes from confronting new and difficult life challenges. Yet evidence is growing that people are experiencing too much stress in modern society. Medical researchers are beginning to link disease to excessively stressful life styles, and psychiatric couches are full of people caught in a web of anxiety from which they are trying to flee.

WHY EXCESS STRESS

Why are so many individuals experiencing excessive stress? Why has what seems to be a natural and healthy response to challenge turned into something that is dangerous to one's health and well being? Herbert Benson (1975) in his book, *The Relaxation Response,* offered a helpful explanation. According to Benson the natural "fight and flight" mechanism that has been passed down to us through evolution is no longer functional. This response, which involves a kind of general body arousal to any kind of threat, originally evolved as a mechanism to help our ancestors meet *physical* challenges through fighting or fleeing. If a caveman were threatened by a giant prehistoric creature, he needed to be able to fight or flee with as much strength or speed as he could muster. In modern civilization individuals are more likely to be threatened psychologically and often do not have the option to fight or flee. Instead they must stay and cope with the situation.

When your boss comes in to give you an unfair assignment, you may feel like fighting or fleeing; but if you value your job, you listen intently. As you listen, you probably are experiencing the physical arousal that accompanies the "fight and flight" mechanism. Because you cannot take any kind of physical action, the energy generated by the "fight and flight" arousal response has no where to go. Benson (1975) contended that this kind of internalization can lead to high blood pressure and other negative physical responses.

Whether or not you agree with this explanation of the human stress mechanism, you should examine carefully the mounting evidence that excessive stress is dangerous. A detailed examination of the effects of excessive stress is included later in the chapter.

BASIC DEFINITION OF
STRESS AND ANXIETY

In this manuscript the terms "stress" and "anxiety" often are used interchangeably to describe reactions to real or to imagined threatening situations. You could say that you are feeling anxiety about a difficult situation at work, or that you are feeling stress about grades at school. Technically, the term "stress" refers to the physical part of an anxiety reaction (muscle tension, increased heart rate and breathing, and so forth); while the term "anxiety" is more general, in that it encompasses both the physical and emotional aspects of the reactions.

OTHER PERSPECTIVES ON ANXIETY

In addition to the basic definition, a number of other perspectives on anxiety provide useful information about the concept. Spielberger (1975) has divided anxiety into two categories, "state" and "trait" anxiety.

Trait anxiety (A-Trait) refers to relatively stable individual differences in anxiety proneness, i.e., to differences among people in their disposition or in their tendency to perceive a wide range of situations as threatening and to respond to these situations with different elevations in state anxiety. . . . Anxiety as an emotional state (A-State) is characterized by subjective, consciously perceived feelings of tension, apprehension, and nervousness accompanied by or associated with activation of the autonomic nervous system. (Spielberger, 1975, p. 137)

6

This view of anxiety differentiates between anxiety that is related to specific situations, and anxiety that is related to a specific personality trait.

Wolpe (1973) took a somewhat different view. He defined "neurotic" anxiety as unrealistic fear. All anxiety in this view is situation-specific in that a stimulus always precipitates an anxiety reaction. The reaction is called "anxiety" only if the fear is unrealistic. For example, if your car is out of control sliding on a sheet of ice, fear is a realistic reaction. If you are afraid to talk with someone at a party, you are experiencing anxiety because this situation cannot really harm you. In this view fear and anxiety are differentiated, although the psychological arousal to both is similar. In terms of the definition used in this book, both fear (reactions to realistic threats) and anxiety (reaction to unrealistic threats) are classified as anxiety.

Holmes and Rahe (1967) viewed stress from a perspective of the stressful events taking place in a person's life. They developed the Social Readjustment Scale, a list of common stressful life events with numerical values related to the amount of stress that each usually produces. An individual can add his/her score on this list to predict the likelihood of stress related diseases within the next year. In this approach an underlying assumption is that anxiety accumulates. After a certain amount of anxiety accumulates from various life events, the effects are felt in terms of disease-proneness.

Anxiety also can accumulate over shorter time periods like a day or a week. In this kind of accumulation, individual anxiety events build your level of tension and thereby lower your threshold for coping with stressful events. For example, if you have just been "chewed out" by your boss, received an angry phone call from a business associate, learned that your son has been suspended from school for truancy, and suddenly realized that you cannot finish the project you are working on by the deadline—your anxiety probably is accumulating. The probability that you will overreact to the next stressor you encounter is high.

Anxiety however cannot be viewed only in the context of reactions to specific situations. Sometimes anxiety seems to be unrelated to any specific situation. You may have heard this kind of anxiety called *free floating* anxiety. Often a general feeling of anxiety is related to what is happening in your life, but it has no immediate or obvious antecedents. People who have a high trait anxiety, as defined by Spielberger (1975), may be more likely to experience these free floating or chronic kinds of stress reactions.

7

EFFECTS OF EXCESSIVE STRESS

At some point when you are thinking about your own anxiety you have to decide what *excessive* means for you. Some anxiety is growth producing and useful, and at times the "fight and flight" mechanism is helpful. Yet many people obviously are encountering the negative effects of too much stress. The following discussion of how excessive anxiety can affect people may help you gain a better understanding of what excessive anxiety means for you.

Impeded Performance

One becomes aware of excessive anxiety most easily when it interferes in some way with the performance of a task. Test anxiety, speech anxiety, and interpersonal anxiety are classic examples. In these situations some anxiety is helpful. The athlete, for example, performs best when he/she is "keyed-up" to perform. Or a student does well on a test because he/she is "psyched" for it. However, too much anxiety impedes the athlete's performance or decreases the student's ability to perform on the test.

The relationship between functional and dysfunctional anxiety is described graphically in Figure 1.1. Before point A the level of anxiety is increasing and performance is also increasing. At point A performance peaks and anxiety continues to increase. Finally after point A an excess of anxiety clearly causes performance to decrease. For example, imagine that you are about to give a speech. As you walk to the podium you feel a bit nervous, but your mind is clear and you feel a surge of energy and power (area before A). As you arrive at the podium and look at the audience, your anxiety begins to get the best of you (point A). As you begin to speak your hands shake, your voice falters, and you begin to talk too quickly (after point A).

Restricted Choices

Sometimes fear of a particular situation becomes so great that a person avoids being in that situation at all costs. If you have to go through life avoiding certain situations because they are too anxiety provoking, you are restricting your life choices.

Consider for example a person who is extremely afraid of flying. (This kind of strong, unexplained fear is called a phobia.) He/she may have to choose a career that does not require flying. Perhaps, if he/she is in the business world, his/her possibilities for advancement will be

8

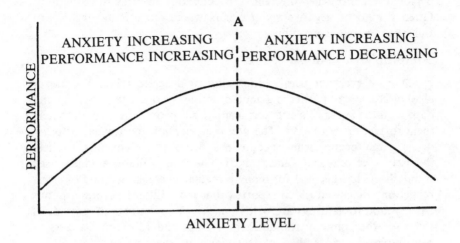

A = Point where performance peaks and increased anxiety reduces performance.

Figure 1.1 Graphical relationship between functional anxiety—anxiety level and performance.

limited. Or, consider the person who is so uncomfortable and anxious when meeting new people that he/she avoids parties or any situations that require him/her to encounter someone new. Naturally his/her universe of possible friends is limited greatly.

Physical Ailments

Although many of the possible physical effects of anxiety tend to be long-term (i.e., heart disease), there are a number of relatively immediate physical effects. These effects include tension headaches, diarrhea and intestinal cramping, nausea, stomach cramps, and stiff/tight muscle groups (neck, jaws, back, etc.). These short-term symptoms may or may not lead to long-term physical problems; however, in themselves they are uncomfortable and undesirable.

Poor Self-Concept and Self-Confidence

People who frequently are anxious and who worry excessively often do not think much of themselves. Over a period of time anxiety limits a person's accomplishments and one gradually comes to feel less capable than other people. This lack of self-confidence makes the overly anxious person even more nervous and self-conscious in stressful situations. Often a kind of negative *spiral* occurs where anxiety and feelings of failure exacerbate each other.

Alcohol/Drug Abuse

Almost everyone uses various kind of drugs to relax. The use of alcohol at cocktail parties is a good example. In order to loosen up and cope with the stress of a stiff social situation, people use alcohol to help them to feel more relaxed. The *abuse* of alcohol, marijuana, or other drugs often occurs when people use drugs too frequently to help themselves become calm and relaxed. The drug Valium, a widely used tranquilizer, has become for many a regular chemical method of stress reduction. Blackwell (1975) reported that 144 million new prescriptions for psychothropic drugs are written each year, with over 50 percent of these for the common tranquilizers Valium and Librium. Dangers of psychological and/or physical dependence on these drugs are great.

Weight Control Problems

Anxiety also is a frequent component of weight control problems. Anxiety sometimes leads to a feeling of nausea and loss of appetite. In the extreme, weight loss and poor nutrition can result. Paradoxically, anxiety also can lead to overeating. For some people the process of eating provides a sense of well-being and calmness; consequently, they try to eat their tension away.

Life Threatening Diseases

A number of diseases have been related to stress, but direct causal relationships have not been established. Pelletier (1977, p. 6) described the following four diseases as "the afflictions of civilization, they are cardiovascular disorders, cancer, arthritis and respiratory diseases (including bronchitis and emphysema)." He considered psychosocial stress a major contributing factor in these diseases. According to Pelletier (1977) most medical textbooks attribute anywhere from 50 to 80 percent of all diseases to psychosomatic or stress related origins. Benson (1975) called hypertension (high blood pressure) the "hidden epidemic." From 15 to 33 percent of the American population suffer from it, and diseases of the heart and brain (related to high blood pressure) account for over 50 percent of the deaths in the United States.

One may be experiencing harmful levels of stress without negative effects on performance. For example, you may be a very good student or business executive who performs well and still be experiencing considerable anxiety. The area left of point A on the Anxiety Performance Graph (Figure 1.1) represents this kind of anxiety. This anxiety is dangerous because in fact it may be helpful to performance. Perhaps the student who constantly is anxious, but who does very well academically uses his/her anxiety to maintain a high level of motivation and commitment. A difficult paradox exists in this kind of situation. Anxiety responses are functional, at least in terms of helping the individual achieve; however, the stress also may be harmful in the long-term because of the potential contribution to the probability of serious diseases like cancer and cardiovascular problems. This paradox seems to be present in a number of high pressure, highly rewarding careers and activities. Remember, also, that what may be a dangerous level of anxiety for one person may not be harmful for someone else.

SUMMARY

1. Stress is a necessary natural response if an individual is to grow and confront new life challenges.

2. The "fight and flight" mechanism involves a kind of physical arousal to threat that is no longer as functional as it was during the earlier part of man's evolution.

3. The terms "stress" and "anxiety" often are used interchangeably to represent a combined emotional and physiological state.

4. Anxiety is related to environmental stimuli, but individuals vary greatly in the degree of anxiety they experience from similar stressors.

5. Effects and experiences of stress can be cumulative.

6. Anxiety is not necessarily related to a specific event. Some individuals experience free floating anxiety and others create anxiety by imagining stressful situations or outcomes.

7. Some environmental factors are unchangeable however most people can alter significantly their reaction to these situations.

8. The determination of what excessive anxiety means must be made individually. What is excessive for one person may not be to another.

9. Excessive stress can lead to the following: (a)restricted life choices, (b) physical ailments, (c) alcohol/drug abuse, (d) weight control problems, (e) low self-concept, and (f) life threatening diseases.

10. High achievers in our society may use stress as a way of motivating themselves and because of their success remain unaware of long-term negative effects.

SELF-ASSESSMENT
DISCUSSION QUESTIONS

1. Describe one or two instances when you experienced the "fight and flight" response. What was the effect on your body? Your mood?

2. When are you apt to use a drug (alcohol, tranquilizers, and so forth) to help you relax? Why?

3. Do you believe that some individuals have personality traits that predispose them to be anxious? Why or why not?

4. How do you think excessive stress affects you?

5. Can you name a career or life style that seems to require a person to experience stress in order to be successful?

6. Do you agree with the idea that anxiety can be harmful even if it does not interfere with your performance?

7. When you are feeling anxious and nervous, how do these affect your self-confidence?

8. Differentiate between the situational and the long-term effects of stress. Can you give a personal example of each?

9. Would you call yourself a nervous or anxious person? Why or why not?

BIBLIOGRAPHY

Benson, H. *The relaxation response.* New York: William Morrow, 1975.

Blackwell, B. Minor tranquilizers, misuse or overuse? *Psychosomatics,* January-February, 1975, *16,* 28-31.

Holmes, T. H., & Rahe, R. H. The social adjustment rating scale. *Journal of Psychosomatic Research.* 1967, *11,* pp. 213-218.

Pelletier, K. R. *Mind as healer, mind as slayer.* New York: Dell Publishing Co., 1977.

Spielberger, C. D., & Sarason, I. G. (Eds.). *Stress and anxiety* (Vol. I). Washington, D.C.:   Hemisphere Publishing, 1975.

Wolpe, J. *The practice of behavior therapy* (2nd ed.). New York: Pergamon Press, 1973.

Walking in the mountains can be a powerful anxiety management technique.

Chapter 2

FOUNDATIONS FOR ANXIETY MANAGEMENT

We live in a complex and stressful world. Anxiety, tension, and worry all seem to be a part of modern life. Yet, each of us has the power to decrease much of the stress in our life. Stress is *manageable*. A number of encouraging approaches to the reduction of anxiety have been developed and researched in recent years. In fact, one difficulty facing a person who is trying to learn to manage stress is the multitude of approaches and techniques available. Enthusiasts embracing techniques from jogging to bioenergetics claim they have the answer.

NEED FOR DIFFERENT APPROACHES AND TECHNIQUES

No single answer for anxiety management is available. The process of anxiety is different for each individual. Some people create much of their anxiety by worrying. You may know someone who manages to worry about almost everything. Other individuals have seemingly automatic anxiety reactions to specific stimuli. This kind of phobic reaction includes things such as fear of snakes, elevators, and flying. Still other individuals seem to be generally nervous and high strung most of the time. For them anxiety seems to be a personality trait.

15

Not only do individuals experience anxiety in different ways, but the same individual also can experience anxiety in different ways at different times. To complicate things even further, the different ways of experiencing anxiety are related to each other.

If you accept the idea that the experience of anxiety is a complex and individualized process, then a multifaceted approach to managing anxiety makes sense. By understanding different approaches and learning techniques to be employed, you increase your chances for success. Just as you can increase your understanding of history by studying it from several different perspectives, you can increase your understanding of anxiety management by examining different approahces. In Chapters 4 through 12 these different approaches and techniques will be discussed in detail.

THREE FOCUS AREAS FOR ANXIETY MANAGEMENT APPROACHES

Helpful to you will be the division of anxiety management approaches into three focus areas: (1) body, (2) mind, and (3) life style. Think about your own anxiety for a moment from these three different perspectives. How do you experience stress in your body? What roles do thinking and worrying play for you? And finally, how does your life style (family, friends, work, play, and so forth) relate to your own anxiety? As in most attempts to categorize human behavior, this scheme is an over-simplification. However, this division can provide a useful framework which will help you understand different anxiety management approaches and their interconnections.

Body

Anxiety effects the human body in a variety of ways. Because of the "fight and flight" mechanism the body responds to threat (real or imagined) by a general arousal—muscles tense, blood flows faster, and breathing increases. Individuals experience these physical responses as part of their anxiety reactions. Pelletier (1977) hypothesized a kind of feedback mechanism that increases arousal if no physical action is taken as a result of anxiety. Thus, if one feels anxious, but does not cope with a physical situation (run, fight) the brain automatically calls for heightened arousal thereby making a person feel even more physical stress.

16

You can decrease the physical tension and stress that accompany anxiety by good nutrition, regular exercise, and various physical relaxation techniques. These techniques work in two ways. The short-term effect usually allows you to control physical tension and therefore perform at a higher level. If you can, for example, give a speech without a shaky voice or without the panic which causes you to forget what you want to say, you have managed your anxiety well. The long-range effects are probably more significant. The regular practice of these techniques will allow you to decrease your overall level of tension and thereby be calm and relaxed. This general decrease in tension level will make you more healthy physically and psychologically.

Chapters 4 and 5 provide techniques for three different methods of physical relaxation: meditation, progressive muscle relaxation, and cue-controlled relaxation. Another major approach to physical relaxation which will not be discussed in these chapters is biofeedback. In this method a person is hooked to a machine that monitors either heart rate, blood pressure, perspiration rate, muscle tension, or brainwave activity. Information is fed back to the person, and by receiving the direct feedback he/she can learn to control the particular response and thereby to relax.

Nutritional and exercise habits (Chapter 6) also are key factors in reducing physical tension. Your diet has a greater effect on your anxiety level than you realize. Caffeine can increase anxiety considerably. Regular exercise provides an outlet for physical tension. You may know individuals (or you may be one) who exercise daily and who feel calmer and at the same time more energetic.

Mind

Most people spend a considerable amount of time talking to themselves. Usually, they do not verbalize what they are thinking, but they still say things to themselves. What they say to themselves affects their behavior, feelings, and specifically their anxiety level. Most people do not realize how much their self-statements can influence anxiety levels both positively and negatively.

In the cognitive (mind) approach to anxiety management you examine and modify thoughts that create or increase anxiety. Two general

17

approaches are used. The first one focuses on beliefs and assumptions that create anxiety. These beliefs are not always easy to identify, and because they often have been with you for a long time it takes considerable effort to change them. Albert Ellis (1977), in his theory of Rational Emotive Psychotherapy, discussed these beliefs and assumptions and how they cause anxiety and other negative feelings and behaviors.

The second approach to modifying anxiety producing thoughts focuses on self-statements that are used to cope with specific stress situations. Meichenbaum (1977) described a technique for coping called "stress-inoculation." This technique involves the development of a series of positive coping self-statements that can be used to help alleviate anxiety related to any difficult stress situation. The focus is on your immediate thoughts and statements, rather than on the more basic beliefs and assumptions that Ellis discussed.

Life Style

The way you choose to live your life affects the amount of anxiety you experience. No matter how positive you learn to be in your thinking or how well you learn to relax, the world that you encounter outside of yourself is important. The term "life style" is an attempt to characterize the type of environment people choose for themselves. If you choose to be a police officer, that affects your life style. If you choose to be a married person, that affects the type of experiences you will encounter. Because a person's life style is complex and consists of hundreds of choices and influences, only four of the most important aspects of life style will be discussed::n personal values, time use, interpersonal relationships, and life transitions.

Anxiety is, of course, not caused by your *values;* but confused values or values that are disregarded can create anxiety. If you always have wanted to pursue an interest in art, but because of practicality you studied engineering, you frequently may experience the general dissatisfaction that comes from failure to follow your inner direction. With the multitude of social, economic, and personal pressures it often is difficult to decide what you want out of life. Assessing your values is a start.

Your perception and *use of time* affect your anxiety level. If you always are rushing to cram one more thing into your life, you probably will experience considerable anxiety. Friedman and Roseman (1974) in

18

their book, *Type A Behavior and Your Heart,* characterized this rushing as a pattern marked by what they called, "hurry sickness." They defined "Type A Behavior" as a distinct behavior pattern that is correlated with a high incidence of heart disease. One way to deal with "hurry sickness" is to examine how you manage and organize time. In general, effective time managers find more time for relaxation, exercise, and recreation. Although the most relaxing way to approach time is to be easy-going and relatively unconcerned, many of the demands of society make some kind of time management a necessity.

People, you cannot live with them and you cannot live without them. *Interpersonal relationships,* interacting with human beings, can at times be a stress provoking activity. Conflicts are part of living with people, as are fears of being hurt and sensitivity to others. Relationships, though, are also a source of great strength. Often by letting off steam or sharing your fears with a loved one, you are able to bring things into perspective and to decrease anxiety. Examining your relationships and your general style of relating to others can help you learn to manage interpersonal anxiety better.

Many transitions occur in life. People constantly are growing and changing, partly as a result of differences inside themselves, and partly as a result of society placing new and different demands upon them. When children become adolescents and begin to mature physically, they develop adult sexual feelings and are *expected* by society to act differently. When adults are in their sixties and lose their spouses and become a widow or widower, a major life change is thrust upon them and they must cope. Many of the anxieties caused by life transitions are difficult to overcome and require much attention and energy. An understanding and acceptance of these transitions coupled with an active approach to the necessary life changes can help decrease the accompanying anxiety.

INTERACTION AMONG BODY, MIND, AND LIFE STYLE

How are these different anxiety management areas interrelated? Your life style and what you choose to include in your life affects what you think and how you react emotionally and physically. You also think about your body reactions. For example, when you become aware of tension in your neck, that means something to you. The complexity of the process and the way that cognitive and emotional reactions interact with each other and with specific life situations makes managing anxiety difficult. Usually you cannot concentrate just on one management area (See Figure 2.1). As you will learn in the next chapter, you need an awareness of how your individual anxiety process works. Then you can use the kind of stress management techniques that make sense for you. Improvement in one area very often helps you in others. The following two examples help illustrate how interactions work for individuals.

Example 1. *Ted, a young business executive, gets very anxious whenever he has to fly in an airplane. He has strong physiological reactions, including fast heart beat, quickened breathing, and stomach cramps whenever he gets near an airplane. His fear of flying might be called a phobic reaction because it is automatic and unrealistic (flying is not particularily dangerous), and because Ted cannot explain why he is so tense and anxious about flying. Because of this strong physiological response, Ted spends much of his time worrying about the fact that he has to make business trips that involve flying. This worrying often results in physiological stress responses just because of his thinking about flying. He has then a kind of escalation with his phobic responses and his worry building on each other to escalate his anxiety feelings. Ted's life style also is involved. He has chosen a career that requires flying periodically, perhaps as a way of trying to force himself to overcome his anxiety. In this case there is an interaction between Ted's phobic response (body), his thinking about the phobic response (mind), and his life style (a job requiring flying).*

Example 2. *Susan, an achievement oriented college student, always feels there is not enough time in a day for her to do everything. She is running constantly from place to place, going to meetings, attending lectures, and trying to maintain a relationship with her friends. Her activity is fine, except that she has a serious colitis problem, and often experiences pain and cramping from it. Her busy schedule and hurried life style seem to create stress. Susan also has a very strong need to achieve and she has come to believe that in order to be worthwhile she has to achieve a great deal. In fact, this assumption is directly tied to her frantic life style.*

One can understand how Susan's basic assumptions (mind) help her create a *life style* that results in a serious physical problem, colitis (body).

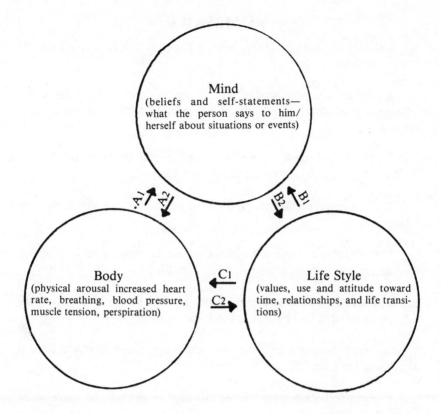

Examples

A1 Awareness of tension creates additional worry (shaking hands made you worry even more about giving a speech)

A2 Thoughts and beliefs effect physical arousal (worry about a new job produces stomach cramps)

B1 Life style issues cause worry (decision to accept a new and difficult responsibility)

B2 Worry or belief produces life style problem (belief that you have to prove yourself causes you to try to do too many things)

C1 Life style issues cause anxiety arousal (inability to be assertive in relationships causes high blood pressure, general muscle tension)

C2 Physical symptoms that affect life style (excessive sweating of palms causes an individual to avoid sexual relationships)

Figure 2.1. Interaction Among Body, Mind, and Life Style.

SUMMARY

1. Different anxiety management techniques can help eliminate excessive anxiety.

2. Anxiety is experienced differently by different individuals; consequently, a multidimensional (focus) approach to anxiety management is necessary.

3. One useful model of anxiety management involves focusing on three intervention areas: body, mind, and life style.

4. Deep muscle relaxation and meditation are ways to learn physical relaxation.

5. Biofeedback is also a useful technique, but muscle relaxation and meditation can provide a similar relaxed state.

6. Exercise and nutritional habits are extremely important considerations related to physical tension and anxiety.

7. Your assumptions about life and your place in it are related directly to your experience of anxiety.

8. Your self-statements during stressful situations can increase or diminish anxiety.

9. The choices you make about how you live and the type of surroundings that you encounter strongly influence anxiety.

10. Although life style includes hundreds of different aspects, a focus on personal values, time use, interpersonal relationships, and life transitions is particularily useful.

11. Although a model of anxiety with management focus areas—body, mind, and life style is helpful, one also must realize that complex interactions occur among the processes in each area.

12. What people feel physically affects what they think, and what they think affects what they feel. What one thinks and feels affects life style choices and life style choices affect what one thinks and feels.

SELF-ASSESSMENT
DISCUSSION QUESTIONS

1. How do you differentiate between acceptable and excessive stress?

2. What methods do you currently use to manage your own excessive anxiety?

3. Do you agree with the statement that individuals experience stress in different ways?

4. Do the three focus areas of anxiety management seem logical to you?

5. Do you think your experience of anxiety is related more to thoughts, body feelings, or life style?

6. Can you identify how the three different areas interact in your experience of anxiety?

7. Can you think of times when you feel physiological stress as a kind of automatic reaction? Can you think of other times when you worry yourself into anxiety?

8. Can you identify a family member or close friend who experiences anxiety very much like you do? Very differently?

9. Has the relative importance of body, mind, and life style changed for you during the last ten years?

10. Have you had any recent life style changes that have affected your anxiety level?

ACTIVITIES

These activities can be completed in conjunction with a class or workshop, or by individuals working independently. More learning will take place if you find some way of discussing what you are learning with other people. If you are not going through this program with a group, you might want to find someone who also is interested in the topic and work through the book as partners, stopping to discuss the questions and activities at the end of each chapter.

Activity 2.1 INTERACTIONS

Purpose: To examine relationships among anxiety processes and experience in the three focus areas.

Instructions: On a blank sheet of paper make three columns headed body, mind, and life style. List several examples of your own anxiety process in each area. For example

body—tense neck or fast breathing

mind—worry about grades or negative thoughts about the future

life style—attending school or working at a hectic job.

After you have several items in each list, draw lines to connect aspects of your anxiety that are related. For example

tense neck—worry about grades—attending school.

Discuss your results with your work group or a friend.

Activity 2.2   TECHNIQUES OF MANAGING ANXIETY

Purpose: To identify anxiety management techniques currently used.

Instructions: Using the same three column sheet or an additional one, list the ways that you currently manage your anxiety in the three areas. For example

body—play softball, take naps

mind—try not to worry, think positively

life style—limit activities, insure time for recreation.

Do not worry if you do not have many current ways to manage anxiety. After you finish with this book, you will have dozens.

BIBLIOGRAPHY

Benson, H. *The relaxation response.* New York: William Morrow, 1975.

Ellis, A. *Reason and emotion in psychotherapy.* New York: Lyle Stuart, 1962. Paperback edition, New York: Citadel, 1977.

Friedman, M., & Rosenman, R. H. *Type A behavior and your heart.* New York: Alfred A. Knopf, Inc., 1974.

Meichenbaum, D. (Ed.). *Cognitive behavior modification: An integrative approach.* New York: Plenum Press, 1977.

Pelletier, K. R. *Mind as healer, mind as slayer.* New York: Dell Publishing Co., 1977.

Chapter **3**

BECOMING AWARE
OF YOUR ANXIETY

One must recognize anxiety before it can be managed. Most people are aware of intense anxiety reactions: they feel their heart pounding when confronting a close friend; or they feel themselves perspiring profusely when going to ask the boss for a raise. A person, however, often is not aware of less intense anxiety reactions. Little things that are annoying throughout the day can build tension levels before they are noticed. Regular irritations or worries can become so commonplace that one no longer realizes how anxiety producing these irritations have become.

The complexity of anxiety also can make it difficult to identify. Awareness is not just recognizing the feeling of butterflies in your stomach. Understanding and recognizing situational stressors, physiological responses, associated thoughts and fantasies, related feelings, accompanying behavior, and blocked and delayed reactions also are involved in the process of awareness.

Reasons are numerous of why you might not be aware of your anxiety process. You may be *blocking* your awareness by a defense mechanism like denial or repression, or you may just lack awareness of the physical effects of anxiety. You also may just not have a clear idea of what an anxiety state involves in comparison to other emotional states like anger, excitement, or sadness.

IMPORTANCE OF AWARENESS
AND UNDERSTANDING

Awareness of your own anxiety is a crucial step if you are to learn to manage your anxiety better. Being aware can help you identify early signals of anxiety, thereby giving you an opportunity to control your reactions in some way. Awareness also allows a kind of anticipation and perhaps a preventive approach. If you know that you have a busy day ahead with a number of activities that particularily are stress provoking, you might _modify_ your schedule because of awareness of your anxiety reactions.

An understanding of how your anxiety reactions work also can be very helpful. Recall, for a moment, the three anxiety management focus areas: body, mind, and life style. If you can develop increased awareness of your own anxiety process in each of these areas, you will be able to use management techniques focusing on a particular area. You also will be able to understand better how your physical and emotional anxiety reactions interact and how they both are related to your life style.

INCREASING YOUR AWARENESS

The best way to increase awareness and understanding of your own anxiety is to examine your feelings of anxiety in a systematic way. You are more apt to discover things you do not know if you ask yourself questions from several different perspectives.

Stressful Situations

A good place to begin is with an identification of situational variables. Do certain situations cause anxiety for you? Do you feel nervous only when you are in an elevator above the seventeenth floor by yourself, or do you experience anxiety whenever you have to disagree with your boss? Granted, you may find difficulty in producing a neat list of all the situations within which you feel anxiety; however, you can learn about which environmental factors are related to stress for you. In assessing your situations, give particular attention to factors such as location, presence/absence of people, time of day, and type of activity.

Feelings of anxiety are _not_ necessarily related to a real life situation. You often may feel anxiety from worrying about imagined situations, present or past. Identifying *both* the real (external) and the imagined (internal) situations is necessary so you can understand better what cues your anxiety. Nearly all anxiety reactions have some kind of cue, although often it is not immediately identifiable.

Take the example of a college student, Bill, who is about to graduate from college. He goes to a counselor reporting that he feels a vague sense of tension and uneasiness. He cannot understand why because he is glad to be leaving college, has a good job offer, and plans to be married in June to a girl he loves. After a few counseling sessions, he realizes that he is worrying about the responsibilities of becoming a husband and a professional. In this case his increased understanding of the reasons (cues) for his feeling anxiety helped him immensely. He was able to talk with a few friends and felt much better when he learned that they too had some fears about leaving school.

Physiological Responses

Because nearly every anxiety reaction has a physiological component, you should know how your body responds to stress.

Physical signs of stress include:

1. increased heart rate
2. muscle tension
   a. forehead
   b. jaw
   c. neck
   d. back
   e. stomach and chest
   f. arms
   g. legs

3. faster breathing
4. perspiration (hands, forehead)
5. higher blood pressure
6. nausea
7. dizziness

The value of increased awareness of these physiological responses makes early detection and intervention possible. If you learn your own

29

physical cues for stress, you will be better able to detect your anxiety reactions. For example, if you are sitting in a small group discussion and you feel a slight tension in your neck and back, that may be a signal to you that you are becoming anxious. Perhaps you want to make a statement, but have not done so. By recognizing an early signal you may be able to use one of the management techniques that you will learn to help relax yourself.

Physical cues also can serve as a warning that your general anxiety level is too high. You may have had to handle a number of small but stress provoking situations in a particular day. When you notice yourself clenching your teeth or moving hurriedly probably you need to *relax* and reduce your general anxiety level. If you can learn to identify the point at which you have accumulated too much stress, you will have come along way in managing your anxiety. Figure 3.1 illustrates how this kind of awareness can work.

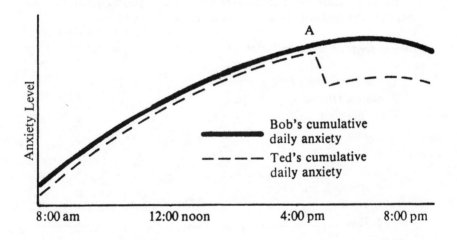

NOTE: At point A at about 4:00 pm Ted became aware of his increasing anxiety level and took fifteen minutes off work to meditate. Bob was not aware of his accumulating anxiety and he therefore did nothing about it. Although Ted's anxiety begins to go up again he winds up the day at an overall lower anxiety level.

Figure 3.1. Awareness of cumulative anxiety.

Thoughts and Fantasies

What do you think or fantasize about when you experience anxiety? Do your thoughts and fantasies cause stress? Do they increase already existing anxiety? Very often a negative interaction occurs between feelings of stress, thoughts, and fantasies. In fact, in later chapters you will be focusing specifically on how your thoughts affect your anxiety. For now however concentrate just on trying to identify what you are saying to yourself that relates to stress. For example, if you are meeting someone important for the first time, do you say things such as, "I'm really nervous, I know I will make a fool out of myself." Or, "I will never get this person to like me, I always clam up when I am nervous." Perhaps you are more positive and say something such as, "Okay, calm down and things will be okay."

What you *think* and *say* to yourself is significant. At times your thoughts probably cue your anxiety and at times they make already existing anxiety worse. An awareness of what you think and say makes possible modification of your self-statements and thoughts in a positive direction.

In addition to thoughts in the form of statements, many individuals fantasize or picture anxiety related situations. You might imagine a scene where you are meeting someone very important and you make a fool out of yourself by going blank and not being able to converse intelligently. Scenes such as this are clues to your fears and tend to make you even more anxious.

Related Feelings

Anxiety often generates other feelings. Individuals sometimes get angry or depressed because they cannot control their anxiety. For example if I have to give a lecture to a large group of people, I might feel anxious and my first few sentences might be shaky and not as decisive as I would like. I could become very angry with myself for not controlling my own anxiety. Or, later that night when I am thinking about the speech, I might become despondent and depressed about the situation.

This kind of negative rebound effect is an important one to identify and understand. Try to figure out if you have a secondary reaction to anxiety. Do you get angry, does your anxiety depress you, or do you feel scared and alone? As you will learn, these negative feelings are **not** a natural outgrowth of anxiety.

Another example of the negative effects of feelings associated with anxiety concerns a young man who is involved in his first sexual experience. Because of feeling anxious about his lack of experience, he is not able to maintain an erection. Although the girl he is with is understanding he feels terribly ashamed, embarrassed, and despondent. These feelings are so strong that he develops an even more intense feeling of anxiety about sexual relationships and is even more anxious during his next sexual encounter.

Related Behavior

Anxiety affects how you behave as well as what you feel. Feelings of stress may be avoided by not following through with certain behaviors. You undoubtedly can think of some tasks, situations, or behaviors you do not do in order to avoid anxiety. At times avoidance has serious consequences. For example, if riding in an automobile is something you avoid in order to escape feelings of anxiety, your life choices are limited significantly.

Anxiety also affects behaviors that cannot be avoided. In these instances excessive stress can interfere with performance. For example, a member of a church choir who is very nervous about performing a solo during the Sunday service may miss several notes because of excessive anxiety. A hostess giving a large dinner party may be so worried about how things are going that she loses some of her coordination and drops gravy on a guest's lap.

Verbal behavior in particular is affected by anxiety. Stuttering, talking loud, talking fast, and going blank are all examples of the effect of stress on verbal communication. Anxiety also seems to effect strongly the way one individual relates to others. A person who is feeling anxious often cannot attend very well to a conversation, he/she is too preoccupied with his/her own anxieties. A person experiencing stress may walk right past a friend and not even recognize him/her. Paying particular attention to the effects of anxiety on interpersonal behavior can be very helpful when trying to understand anxiety feelings.

Blocked and Denied Anxiety

Some individuals do not allow themselves to feel or experience anxiety. This kind of *blocking* of anxiety is a learned defense. Repression and denial are common defense mechanisms used against anxiety. Repression is a kind of automatic forgetting. In this case a person might forget continually how anxious he/she felt in order to escape having to deal with the experience and the consequences. Blocking occurs when one denies the existence of anxiety, perhaps by telling him/herself that he/she is not really nervous, just a little excited. These processes often operate unconsciously, so that after a while the individual is *not aware* of the anxiety.

The difference between managing and blocking anxiety is clear. When you manage your anxiety, you allow yourself to experience anxiety and identify it as a first step in the management process. The underlying assumption is that the experience of anxiety is a natural human response that can be managed. When you block your experience of anxiety by defense mechanisms such as repression or denial, you are not allowing yourself to be consciously aware of your anxiety; and therefore, your possibilities for effectively managing anxiety are limited. Blocking is not an effective management technique. Although the feelings and experiences are blocked, your body probably still is reacting in some way. The possibility is strong that some kind of physical stress reaction is occuring. This unnoticed reaction helps explain why people who are not aware of anxiety have stress related difficulties such as ulcers, colitis, and headaches.

Your external behavior also may be affected by blocked anxiety. That is, you may not realize you are anxious or tense, yet you may avoid certain situations or respond as if you were threatened. By becoming aware of your own anxiety you have a much better chance of modifying anxiety related behaviors that are troublesome. If you know that you get very anxious when too many demands are placed upon you, you can anticipate this reaction and perhaps modify your situation. If you really do not understand what is happening, you are apt to accept too many obligations continually, probably not meeting them because of anxiety. Ultimately negative attitudes can be developed toward yourself because you cannot satisfy all the demands.

Delayed Reactions

Your reactions to and about anxiety may be delayed. For example, you may not realize until the end of the day how angry you are at yourself for letting anxiety prevent your participation in a discussion on an important subject. Or, it may not be until you look back over a period of time that you begin to realize how anxious and nervous you really were for the entire period.

In a way, delayed reactions are extremely helpful. They allow you to feel and to experience things with which you may have been unable to deal earlier. Delayed reactions also can provide valuable information about the anxiety process. By attending to your delayed reactions and trying to make some sense out of them, you can gain valuable insights into your anxiety process.

Leslie is a good example. She is the type of person who jokes around very much. She never takes things too seriously and is always making jokes and cheering up her friends. However, an upsetting thing happened with one of her best friends. This friend was feeling very depressed and when he tried to talk with Leslie, she immediately launched into a long and very funny story about a recent experience. The two friends parted company with her friend smiling. She noticed at the time that she felt great relief after he left. Later that day as she was thinking about her friend she realized how afraid she was of responding to his depression. She began to feel that same fear and also sadness because she had not been able to respond to him. The value of this delayed reaction was that it helped Leslie learn about a typical interpersonal anxiety of hers, her fear of responding to people's negative feelings.

By taking this first step and becoming more aware of your own anxiety mechanisms you are paving the way for more effective anxiety management. Awareness itself can become an anxiety management technique. Certainly learning the early warning cues of stress reactions can give you a chance to prevent or avert more serious stress reactions. Increased awareness, coupled with the techniques introduced in the following chapters, will give you powerful tools to combat and to manage unwanted tension and anxiety.

SUMMARY

1. Understanding how your own anxiety reactions typically work is extremely helpful.

2. You should try to identify the stimulus situations which seem to create stress for you. These situations can be internal or external.

3. Internal physiological responses such as increased heart rate, muscle tension, or faster breathing are signs of anxiety.

4. An awareness of these physiological signs of anxiety can allow you to identify more accurately your own anxiety levels.

5. Thoughts and fantasies often are related to stressful situations. These thoughts and fantasies may be important in causing or increasing anxiety.

6. Experience of anxiety often is accompanied by other feelings such as anger or despair.

7. Anxiety often negatively effects performance or prevents one from carrying out a desired task or behavior.

8. Verbal behavior and communication with others is affected strongly by anxiety.

9. Blocking anxiety feelings by denying them or by not allowing yourself to be aware of them is *not* an effective stress management technique.

10. Blocking anxiety feelings does not prevent negative physiological and behavioral effects.

11. Delayed reactions to anxiety offer information that previously was not available to the conscious mind.

12. A better understanding and awareness of personal anxiety mechanisms is in itself a useful anxiety management technique.

SELF-ASSESSMENT
DISCUSSION QUESTIONS

1. How do you first become aware of anxiety?

2. Is anxiety cumulative for you? (Does anxiety increase over the course of a day for example?)

3. Is an anxiety stimulus situation necessarily an external event?

35

4. What is an example of an internal stimulus situation?

5. How are internal physiological responses such as high blood pressure or quickened heart beat related to anxiety?

6. Where do you most frequently feel muscle tension as a result of stress?

7. Describe a fantasy that might be related to stress. Give an example from your own life.

8. What thoughts do you have when you feel anxious?

9. Do you think that thoughts cause anxiety or vice versa? Can you give examples?

10. How might feelings like anger or despair be related to stress?

11. Why would someone get angry at himself/herself for experiencing anxiety?

12. In what ways can behavior be affected by anxiety?

13. How can an understanding of delayed responses to anxiety be useful?

14. During your average day when does your anxiety curve reach its peak?

15. When would you be most likely to get in touch with your own delayed reactions to anxiety?

16. What is meant by blocking or denying anxiety feelings? Why is this harmful?

17. Do you ever deny your anxiety feelings?

ACTIVITIES

Activity 3.1 ANXIETY ASSESSMENT

Purpose: Increase awareness of different aspects of the anxiety process.

Instructions: Keep a journal for a week and write about your anxiety experiences. Try to analyze these different situations by commenting on each of these previously described topics:

Stressful situations

Physiological responses

Thoughts and fantasies

Related feelings

Related behavior

Blocked or denied anxiety

Delayed reactions

Try to think of some generalizations about your own anxiety process. Discuss your ideas with a friend or your group.

Activity 3.2 DAILY ANXIETY GRAPH

Purpose: Assess daily anxiety patterns.

Instructions: Record your level of anxiety over the course of several days. Make for yourself a daily graph similar to the one shown in Figure 3.1. Try to discern patterns and determine your daily high stress points. Compare your pattern with someone else's pattern. How are they different? Similar?

PART II

BODY APPROACHES: PHYSICAL RELAXATION AND HEALTH

PART II

BODY APPROACHES: PHYSICAL RELAXATION AND HEALTH

In Part II the primary focus is on anxiety management approaches that directly effect your physical experience of stress. If you can learn to decrease the negative physical aspects of stress and anxiety, you will have a powerful anxiety management tool. Because of decreased tension and increased energy you will be able to improve your performance in many life areas and you also will be able to gain some control over excessive anxiety in specific situations. By learning to manage the physical aspects of anxiety you also positively influence anxiety that is more closely related to your thinking process and your life style.

In Chapters 4 and 5 you will learn two easy, yet profoundly important ways to manage anxiety. Each of these approaches, meditation and deep muscle relaxation, provides you with a simple but effective way to consistently reduce your daily tension level. Because these techniques have such a strong calming effect on the body, they are included in this section. Actually, meditation is a relaxation technique that begins with a kind of mental relaxing, and even deep muscle relaxation is greatly effected by a person's attitudes and thoughts. Again, the almost inevitable interaction between body, mind, and life style becomes obvious.

Chapter 6 does not contain a specific relaxation technique; the material is rather an attempt to show how important general physical health is to the physical experience of anxiety. Specifically, exercise and nutritional effects of anxiety are explored and suggestions for improvement are offered.

41

You need to be in a comfortable position to meditate.

Chapter 4

MEDITATION/
RELAXATION RESPONSE

If the word meditation conjures up visions of long-bearded gurus walking across hot coals or monks chanting at dawn in cold cells, you have a somewhat stereotyped view of meditation. Although many religions and philosophies include a type of meditation, accepting a specific religious or philosophical orientation is not necessary in order to use meditation as a relaxation technique.

COMMON ELEMENTS

Although meditation has been advocated as a relaxation technique (Benson, 1975) for use in contemporary western societies, its roots go back 2500 years (Pelletier, 1977). A number of different kinds of meditation exist in both eastern and western traditions. Although the form or method may differ, each meditation technique seems to be used to help the meditator transcend his normal state of consciousness. Naranjo and Ornstein (1971) in an excellent book on the psychology of meditation, discussed the common elements found in each of the major eastern meditative traditions, zen, yoga, and sufism:

> The strong common element seems to lie in the actual restriction of awareness to single, unchanging process. It does not seem to matter which actual physical practice is followed: whether one symbol or other is employed; whether the visual system is used

or body movements repeated; whether awareness is focused on a limb or on a sound or on a word or prayer. (Naranjo & Ornstein, 1971, p. 161)

Herbert Benson (1975), in his book *Relaxation Response,* identified four elements common to all types of meditation:

1. quiet environment,
2. mental device,
3. passive attitude, and
4. comfortable position.

Benson quoted a variety of Christian mystics, Eastern religious philosophers, and secular writers to illustrate the universality of these basic elements. The Prayer of Heart described in a compendium of Greek and Byzantine writing incorporates all four of Benson's (1975) elements:

Sit down alone and in silence. Lower your head, shut your eyes, breathe out gently, and imagine yourself looking into your own heart. As you breathe out, say "Lord Jesus Christ, have mercy on me." Say it moving your lips gently, or simply say it in your mind. Be calm, be patient and repeat the process frequently. (Benson, 1975, p. 122)

The passive attitude and use of an object on which to dwell can be seen in a quote from Al-Ghazali, a Sufi Moslem:

And let him see to it that nothing save God most high enters his mind. Then as he sits in solitude, let him not cease, saying continuously with his tongue, "Allah, Allah," keeping his thought on it. At last he will reach a state when the motion of his tongue will cease, and it will seem as though the word flowed from it. Let him persevere in this until all trace of motion is removed from his tongue, and he finds his heart persevering in thought. (Benson, 1975, pp. 131-132)

Wordsworth described "a happy stillness of mind," and a "central peace subsisting forever at the heart of endless agitation." In "Tintern Abbey" he wrote:

. . . that serene and blessed mood,

In which . . . the breath of his corporeal frame,

And even the motion of our human blood,

Almost suspended, we are laid asleep

In body, and become a living soul:

While with an eye made quiet by the power

Of harmony, and the deep power of joy,

We see into the life of things. (Benson, 1975, p. 138)

Kenneth Pelletier (1977) did not agree with Benson's notion of four universal meditative elements. However, he did agree with Benson that the two forms of meditation most widely practiced in Western culture, Zen meditation and Transcendental meditation, induce a general reduction in physiological arousal. This reduction in physiological arousal is what Benson (1975) called the "relaxation response."

BODY RESPONSE

This lowering of arousal is most important in using meditation as an anxiety management technique. Although the more esoteric ideas about altered states of consciousness are fascinating, the important part of meditation for anxiety management purposes is the physical relaxation that it induces. This is not to say an altered mental state, perhaps a more relaxed level of consciousness, is not important. In fact, many meditators report a powerful calming effect on their mind.

What actually happens to your body during meditation or in Benson's (1975) words "relaxation response"? He also reported in a number of studies of the relaxation response the following physiological changes:

1. decreased oxygen consumption,
2. decreased respiratory rate,
3. decreased heart rate,
4. increased alpha waves,
5. decreased blood pressures (in people who have elevated blood pressure), and
6. decreased blood lactate levels.

According to Benson (1975) all of these physiological changes represent a *hypometabolic* state associated with generally decreased activity in the sympathetic nervous system. This state is in direct opposition to the *hypermetabolic* state related to arousal and the "fight and flight" mechanism.

Benson's contention that this relaxation state is a natural counterpart to the "fight and flight" arousal state is interesting. He believes that although a natural relaxation response exists, it is not used very frequently in our culture. Demands for accomplishment and activity make it unusual for a person to sit quietly in a relaxed position. If this natural response exists, and strong evidence suggests that it does, mankind can rediscover a pleasant, simple, and very useful relaxation technique.

MEDITATION AND ANXIETY

If meditation can help you relax and achieve this lowered arousal state, will your anxiety feelings decrease? Yes, in fact the primary value of this technique is as a reducer of cumulative anxiety. Remember that anxiety can build throughout the day, sometimes without your conscious awareness. This unconscious buildup means that you may be physiologically tense and also that you may respond to outside events and pressures with a short fuse. The regular practice of meditation will help you control anxiety and perhaps help and more effectively cope with anxiety producing situations. Pelletier (1977) called this effect a lowering of *stress reactivity*. He also argued that the generally lowered neurophysiological functioning that meditation produces helps you avoid stress related diseases.

Remember, too, that by decreasing your general stress level you may experience a number of related positive changes. Meditators have reported increased energy, better work performance, lower drug and alcohol use, more self-esteem, and more effective interpersonal relationships. If you are interested in more information about the effects of meditation, you may want to read *TM: Discovering Inner Energy and Overcoming Stress* by Harold H. Bloomfield, Peter Cain, and Dennis T. Jaffee, or *Scientific Research on Transcendental Meditation: Collected Papers,* edited by L. Domash, J. Farrow, and D. Orme-Johnson.

LEARNING TO MEDITATE

The relaxation response as defined by Benson (1975) is not difficult to learn and once mastered it is a natural, self-rewarding process. Although meditation can be learned and practiced independently, having supervision by an experienced meditator or teacher is helpful. You probably are more likely to follow through with the regular practice of meditation if you are in some kind of formal training program. In general, getting yourself to practice on a regular basis is more difficult than learning the response itself. The first focus presently will be on learning the relaxation response, and the second on developing a personal plan for the regular practice of meditation.

Directions for Learning to Meditate

Benson (1975) gave four basic directions for cueing the relaxation response:

(1) A Quiet Environment
Ideally, you should choose a quiet, calm environment with as few distractions as possible. A quiet room is suitable, as is a place of worship. The quiet environment contributes to the effectiveness of the repeated word or phrase by making it easier to eliminate distracting thoughts.

(2) A Mental Device (object on which to dwell)

To shift the mind from logical, externally oriented thought, there should be a constant stimulus: a sound, word, or phrase repeated silently or aloud; or fixed gazing at an object. Because one of the major difficulties in the elicitation of the Relaxation Response is "mind wandering," the repetition of the word or phrase is a way to help break the train of distracting thoughts. Your eyes usually are closed if you are using a repeated sound or word; of course, your eyes are open if you are gazing. Attention to the normal rhythm of breathing also is useful and enhances the repetition of the sound of the word.

(3) A Passive Attitude

When distracting thoughts occur, they are to be disregarded and attention redirected to the repetition or gazing; *you should not worry about how well you are performing the technique,*

47

because this may well prevent the Relaxation Response from occuring. Adopt a "let it happen" attitude. *The passive attitude is
perhaps the most important element in elicitng the Relaxation
Response. Distracting thoughts will occur. Do not worry about
them. When these thoughts do present themselves and you
become aware of them, simply return to the repetition of the
mental device. These other thoughts do not mean you are performing the technique incorrectly. They are to be expected.*

(4) A Comfortable Position

A comfortable posture is important so that there is no undue muscular tension. Some methods call for a sitting position.
A few practitioners use the cross-legged "lotus" position of the
Yogi. If you are lying down, there is a tendency to fall asleep. As
we have noted previously, the various postures of kneeling,
swaying, or sitting in a cross-legged position are believed to have
evolved to prevent falling asleep. You should be comfortable
and relaxed. (Benson, 1975, pp. 159-161)

Developing a Plan

One of the real challenges in learning to use meditation is practicing
on a regular basis. Leon Otis (1974) in a *Psychology Today* article,
reported that 50 percent of the people who started transcendental
meditation did not continue. The following suggestions can help you accrue the benefits of relaxation that come from regular and consistent
practice:

1. *Create a satisfactory environment*

Find a place to meditate that you can use consistently. Finding a
quiet spot that is easily available to you may be more difficult than you
think. You may need the cooperation of family, friends, or roommates.
You should not be disturbed and people around you should respect your
need for quiet and privacy. Remember also to turn your telephone off
and put a note on your door if necessary.

2. *Meditate at the same time every day*

Meditating twice a day for ten to twenty minutes generally gives the
best results. Benson (1975) suggested that there may be dangers in

meditating for longer periods; however, he reported finding no negative side effects for people who meditate for ten to twenty minutes twice a day. By meditating at the same time every day you can maximize the conditioning effect. When you sit to meditate in the same location at the same time, you will almost automatically bring forth the relaxation response.

3. *Find your own best time and length of time*

Most people seem to have a meditation cycle that automatically falls between ten and twenty minutes. If you feel like you may fall asleep or meditate longer than twenty minutes, you should wear a watch or have a clock available so that you can glance at the time periodically, or you may want to use a clock radio tuned to a quiet music station to signal when your time is finished. Try to avoid loud noises as they can be quite jarring if you are meditating deeply.

Meditation seems to be easiest and most useful when practiced on an empty stomach. Arranging your meditation times before meals usually is best. The most universally helpful time seems to be before dinner. For most people this is a time when they need to relax and renew themselves after a full day of activity.

4. *Use social reinforcement*

When you are first learning to meditate, it helps to compare your experiences with someone who also is learning. This way the fun and excitment can be shared, and you also can discuss your reactions. Remember, though, not to worry about how well you are meditating. If you find yourself worrying, you have violated the requirement to maintain a passive attitude.

5. *Expect different experiences*

Your meditation experiences will vary. At times you will be conscious of repeating your word or phrase, while at other times you will be totally unaware of them. During some meditations you will have a number of interfering thoughts while at other times your mind will be blank. Sometimes you may be aware of colors or scenes and at other times just blank space. Part of the enjoyment of meditation involves these different experiences, and remember that during all of these *subjective* experiences your body and mind are relaxing.

6. *Do not force meditation*

At times you cannot, or do not feel like meditating. Do not force yourself. Certainly, nothing is wrong with deciding not to meditate on specific occasions. Watch out, though, that you do not begin to find other things to do regularly and lose the meditation habit.

7. *Find time to meditate*

You probably will not find time to meditate unless you are serious about it. Saying you are too busy or forgetting to take the time is easy—you have to make a commitment to yourself and stick to it. After all, spending a few minutes each day with yourself in quiet solitude is not a difficult task, and for those few minutes you can achieve a considerably more relaxed way of living.

SUMMARY

1. Although meditation often is associated with religion, it is possible to use meditation as a relaxation technique without adhering to any particular religious or philosophical principles.

2. Meditation has been practiced for 2500 years in a variety of contexts. It often has been used by practitioners to alter their state of consciousness.

3. Herbert Benson (1975) has identified four common elements in all types of meditation: a quiet environment, an object to dwell on, a passive attitude, and a comfortable position.

4. Evidence for these common elements can be found in the writings of Christian mystics, Eastern religious philosophers, and from secular literature.

5. Benson (1975) described a number of physiological changes associated with meditation which he labels the "relaxation response". These changes all are associated with decreased physical arousal and relaxation.

6. The regular practice of meditation can be a potent anxiety reducer.

7. Pelletier (1977) described a lowering of stress reactivity. This reaction means that meditators will be less likely to react negatively to stressful situations because generally they will be more relaxed.

8. The relaxation response (meditation) is not difficult to learn; however, an experienced teacher is helpful.

9. You may have to take an active role in creating an environment suitable for meditation.

10. Generally, meditating twice a day for periods of 10 to 20 minutes is best. Each person must find his/her own best schedule and time length.

11. Comparing experiences with other people helps to reinforce your practice of meditation.

12. You can expect a variety of different subjective meditation experiences. Try to accept different experiences without evaluating the *quality* of your meditation.

13. Although finding the time to meditate daily may be difficult, it definitely is worthwhile.

SELF-ASSESSMENT
DISCUSSION QUESTIONS

1. Have you experienced anything similar to meditation?

2. What are your attitudes and reactions to the word "meditation"?

3. How would you describe a passive attitude?

4. Would a passive attitude be difficult for you? Why or why not?

5. How can you develop a quiet environment to use for meditation?

6. What would the attitude of your friends and family be about your meditating? Would they be cooperative?

7. Do you find sitting quietly without doing anything difficult?

8. What is meant by a lowering of stress reactivity? What are some ways that you can lower your own stress reactivity?

9. What times of day would be best for you to meditate? Why?

10. How do you feel about the altered state of consciousness that is achieved through meditation?

11. How would you be most likely to avoid meditation?

ACTIVITIES

Activity 4.1 MEDITATION PRACTICE

Purpose: Learn to meditate and thereby produce the relaxation response.

Instructions: Try meditating twice a day for a week. Keep a log of when you meditate and your reactions to each session. Try to describe in a sentence or two your experiences each time you meditate. Try to ascertain over the week whether you feel any different. Is your energy level different? Sleeping habits different? and so forth? Discuss your log with someone who also is learning to meditate.

Activity 4.2 OVERCOMING BLOCKS TO MEDITATION

Purpose: Encourage exploration of potential problems with meditation and development of strategies to overcome these difficulties.

Instructions: After you have learned to meditate and have experimented for a few days, make a list of several potential problems that you perceive might interfere with your practicing meditation on a regular basis (i.e., forget about it, cannot find a place, little brother interrupts me, and so on). Work on developing strategies to overcome these difficulties. Discuss your potential problems with members of your participating group or with a friend.

BIBLIOGRAPHY

Benson, H. *The relaxation response.* New York: William Morrow, 1975.

Bloomfield, H., Cain, P., & Jaffee, D. *TM: Discovering inner energy and overcoming stress.* New York: Delacorte Press, 1975.

Domash, L., Farrow, J., & Orme-Johnson, D. *Scientific research on transcendental meditation.* Los Angeles: Maharishi International University, 1976.

Naranjo, C., & Ornstein, R. E. *On the pyschology of meditation.* New York: Viking, 1971.

Otis, L. S. The facts of transcendental meditation: If well integrated but anxious, try TM. *Psychology Today,* 1974, *7,* 45-46.

Pelletier, K. R. *Mind as healer, mind as slayer.* New York: Dell Publishing Co., 1977.

Deep muscle relaxation involves tensing and then relaxing various muscle groups.

Chapter 5

DEEP MUSCLE
RELAXATION

Have you ever been lying on the beach in the hot sun listening to the gentle sounds of the ocean and silently remarked to yourself that it feels really good to be so relaxed? Your legs and arms seemed to merge into the sand, creating an overall feeling of profound relaxation. If you have not had this experience, you have something for which to look forward, because deep muscle relaxation can provide a similar feeling.

The technique is relatively simple. By learning how to relax various muscle groups in your body, you can create an overall sense of relaxation that in effect melts away your tensions and anxieties. Because of the strong relationship between anxiety and your body, it is impossible to relax your muscles deeply and still to have feelings of tension and anxiety. To state more technically, the muscle relaxation and associated general autonomic relaxation inhibits anxiety.

Edmund Jacobsen (1938; 1964, p. 65), who first described progressive deep muscle relaxation in 1938, also suggested that muscle relaxation helps eliminate residual tension that usually remains during normal periods of rest or sleep. In other words the technique not only helps you relax during the procedure itself, but also helps decrease accumulated tension.

HOW DOES DEEP
MUSCLE RELAXATION WORK?

Deep muscle relaxation consists of tensing and loosening muscle groups throughout the body. The sensation you have after clenching your fist for 15 seconds and then relaxing it is a kind of exaggerated relaxation. Because of the energy you used to clench the muscle in your fist, a period right after the tensing exists when the muscles are in a state of recovery. This state perhaps is akin to some of the moments in life, like the scene on the beach when you feel total relaxation. By systematically tensing and releasing various muscle groups, you create a progression toward this super relaxed state. As you note the difference among tension, your normal state, and this exaggerated relaxation, you gradually will release much of the normal muscle tension that you store throughout your body. If you tend to carry tension in a specific area, you will notice particularly the contrast between tension in the muscle group and the relaxed state. As this progressive deep muscle relaxation begins to overtake you, your mind will become calmer and you will care less about the worries and difficulties which might be present in your mind. Just as the calmness of mind in meditation moves to your body, the relaxation in deep muscle relaxation leads to calmness of mind.

USES OF DEEP MUSCLE RELAXATION

Deep muscle relaxation as an anxiety management technique can be used in two different ways. The first use is much the same as meditation; deep muscle relaxation can be used daily as a relaxation technique. By experiencing deep relaxation once or twice a day you can dramatically reduce your overall anxiety level. In essence, you interrupt the escalating daily stress level (as shown in Figure 3.1). You can accrue the same benefits from using progressive deep muscle relaxation as you can from meditation (relaxation response). You will feel more energetic, yet more relaxed, and your overall approach to life will be more positive.

The second use is called *active* muscle relaxation. The purpose of active muscle relaxation is to provide a quick decrease of tension during particularly difficult situations. If your hand shakes and your mind goes blank during a tough exam, *active* relaxation will help with the immediate tension symptoms (in this case shaking and confusion). Additional instructions for use of this technique will be provided later in the chapter.

MEDITATION VERSUS
DEEP MUSCLE RELAXATION

Because meditation and deep muscle relaxation appear to accomplish similar states of relaxation, it may be useful to differentiate between the two techniques. Some people seem to find one technique better than the other. In a way the relaxation that both techniques produce is a kind of conditioned response that people learn to produce during specific rest periods. For some meditation is easier because it does not involve muscle tensing and releasing. These people tend to achieve the relaxed state more easily through their minds. Muscle relaxation is often preferred by people who have difficulty with meditation or who have specific muscle tension areas. One advantage of the deep muscle relaxation is that it can be modified to help individuals focus on particular physical tension areas.

HOW TO PRACTICE PROGRESSIVE
DEEP MUSCLE RELAXATION

Muscle groups and specific exercises to use in deep muscle relaxation are listed on the following pages. The exercises can be done while sitting in a firm chair or while reclining.

Be careful of injuries such as bad knees, and so forth. Skip a particular muscle group if it is unduly uncomfortable or too much of a strain. The order of exercising muscle groups also can be determined by you—choose one that works best.

As you are tightening and relaxing muscle groups, remember the following:

1. Keep your eyes closed.
2. Sit or lie in a comfortable position.
3. Try to concentrate on the difference between tension and relaxation.
4. Imagine that tension is flowing out of your body.
5. Take deep, relaxing breaths—try to breathe from your abdomen.

You may want to ask someone to give the exercises verbally the first few times, or you can record a relaxation tape and use it for the first several practice sessions. Remember, though, that your ultimate goal is to be able to achieve deep muscle relaxation by yourself.

For each muscle or muscle group you are to tighten a muscle, hold it for 5 to 15 seconds, and then slowly relax the muscle. (Set your own pace, but relax for at least 5 seconds before you proceed to the next muscle.) Repeat the exercises with each muscle and then go to the next one. After you have practiced regularly for a week or two, you will develop a conditioned relaxation response. At that point you can abbreviate the muscle tensing procedures, depending upon how easily you can relax. An abbreviated version also is included.

Specific Muscle Groups

A. *Arms and Shoulders* (As you loosen each muscle, say the word "relax" to yourself and/or exhale.)

1. Clench both fists—note tension in hand and forearm— relax.

2. Touch shoulders with fingers, raise arms—note tension in biceps and upper arms—relax

3. Straighten and strech arms—note tension in tricept muscles along back of arms—relax.

B. *Face, Neck, Shoulders*

1. Wrinkle forehead—note tension around eyes and forehead—relax.

2. Close eyes tightly—note tension—relax with eyes lightly closed.

3. Press tongue into roof of mouth—note tension in mouth—relax.

4. Press lips together tightly—note tension in mouth and chin— relax.

5. Press head backward—note tension in neck and upper back—relax.

6. Push head forward, bury chin in chest—note tension in neck and shoulders—relax.

7. Shrug shoulders, raise as high as possible—note tension in shoulders—relax.

58

C. *Chest, Stomach, and Lower Back*

1. Arch your back, move away from back of chair, push arms backward—note tension in back and shoulder—relax.

2. Take a deep breath and hold it—note tension in chest and back—relax.

3. Take two deep breaths of air, hold, and then exhale—note your breathing becomes slower and more relaxed—relax.

4. Suck in stomach, try to make it reach your spine—note feeling of tension in the stomach—relax, note your breathing becomes more regular.

5. Push out stomach—note tension—relax.

D. *Hips, Thighs, and Calves*

1. Tense buttocks by raising yourself up on them—note tension—relax.

2. Flex thighs by straightening legs—note tension—relax.

3. Point toes toward face—note tension in foot and calves of legs—relax.

4. Curl toes downward as if burying them in sand—note tension in arches of feet—relax.

Abbreviated Version

A. *Combining Muscle Groups*

1. Tense all facial and neck muscles at once (see previous steps B-1 through B-7)—relax.

2. Tense muscles of the arms and trunk (see steps A-1, A-2, A-3, B-1, C-4)—relax.

3. Tense lower body (see steps D-1 through D-4)—relax.

B. *Focus on the Muscle Groups Most Prone to Tension.*

For most people tension tends to center in one or two parts of the body, e.g., neck, stomach, forehead. Relaxing these critical areas can foster general bodily relaxation.

Breathing

When you try the progressive muscle relaxation procedures, you probably will find yourself taking a deep breath whenever you say the word "relax" to yourself. For many of us a deep breath is naturally associated with a sense of relaxation. Ballentine (1976) in a book devoted to the science of breath suggests that extended expiration which comes with deep (diaphragmatic) breathing is associated with parasympathetic tone and relaxation. [Note: Similar muscle relaxation instructions can be found in Jacobsen (1938 and 1964), Kanfer and Goldstein (1975), and Wolpe (1973). Jacobsen (1938) originated the technique.]

Unfortunately most of us tend to breath more quickly and shallowly when we are experiencing anxiety. If you learn to become conscious of your breathing and particulary of shallow breathing, you can help relax yourself by deep breathing.

You can practice deep breathing by lying in a prone position and placing your hand upon your stomach. As you breath, you will feel your stomach filling and emptying. If you consciously breath deeply and exhale slowly, you will begin to feel more and more relaxed. As you focus on your breathing and on the slow and gradual expulsion of air, you will become even more relaxed. This kind of breathing, of course, usually is encouraged as part of progressive deep muscle relaxation.

Relaxation Fantasy

Many practitioners of progressive deep muscle relaxation find it helpful after they have finished the muscle exercises to use a relaxing fantasy for a few minutes. Choose a scene that you can see easily in your mind's eye that you previously have associated with relaxation—A warm day on the beach perhaps, or sitting near a cool mountain stream. The addition of this fantasy often helps people move into an even deeper state of relaxation.

Suggestions

Remember also that if you plan to use deep muscle relaxation as a daily relaxation technique, you need to practice it consistently. Suggestions given for helping establish the regular practice of meditation also apply. A summary of these suggestions follows. For a more thorough review, refer to Chapter 4 on Meditation.

1. Create a satisfactory environment.

2. Try to use the technique at the same time every day.

3. Find your own best variation of the technique.

4. Use social reinforcement.

5. Expect different relaxation experiences.

6. Do not force relaxation.

7. *Find time* to practice deep muscle relaxation.

People frequently learn deep muscle relaxation in a setting where someone with a calm, soothing voice gives them initial instruction. Although this kind of instruction is not necessary, it often facilitates learning because of the calmness of the voice and the continual suggestion by the person to relax.

ACTIVE DEEP MUSCLE RELAXATION

The second use of deep muscle relaxation is to help you cope with *specific* anxiety situations. A number of recent studies have demonstrated that people can be taught to use the deep muscle relaxation technique in specific situations (Deffenbacher, Michaels, Michaels, & Daley, 1980; Goldfried, 1971; Goldfried & Trier, 1974; Suinn & Richardson, 1971).

Active use of muscle relaxation involves the use of a personal *cue* signal that one uses to trigger deep muscle relaxation. For example, imagine signal that you have been asked by a very good friend to lend her $1,000 and you have to call her on the telephone to tell her that you are not willing to make the loan. As you approach the telephone and begin dialing, you become aware of tension in your neck and throat. You realize that you really are very anxious about making the telephone call. If you have learned to use active deep muscle relaxation, you will be able to use your relaxation cue, perhaps a deep breath to signal your body to relax. This response, of course, will be present only if you have learned to relax on cue.

LEARNING ACTIVE
DEEP MUSCLE RELAXATION

The basic requirement is to learn the deep muscle relaxation technique. As you are going through the muscle tensing and relaxing, you should develop a personal signal or cue. Either a deep breath or the word "relax" will serve. You can learn this signal by pairing the word or a deep breath with each muscle relaxation. The idea is to pair the cue with relaxation.

In order to use this active deep muscle relaxation technique you have to be keenly aware of when you become anxious. Your previous work on anxiety awareness will help. Also, as you learn deep muscle relaxation you will become more aware of the physical indications of anxiety. The strength of the relaxation response that you can achieve on cue also is crucial. The more you practice and learn to produce relaxation actively, the easier it will be to relax on cue.

If you want to use deep muscle relaxation to help you deal with specific life situations, you must learn to relax in various settings. Remember that when you initially learned deep muscle relaxation you were in a reclining chair in a quiet environment. Much additional practice is necessary to be able to achieve deep muscle relaxation at work, while talking to your spouse, or while riding in a car. Go back for a moment to the earlier work you did on anxiety awareness. Make a list of the situations that seem to make you anxious, then practice cueing your deep muscle relaxation in a similar setting. Try to arrange a gradual learning progression. For example, if one of your high anxiety situations involves interaction with a co-worker, try cueing deep muscle relaxation at work when the person is not present. Next, try it when the person is present, but not talking to you, and try it when you are having a conversation that is not stressful. Finally, you will be ready to use the technique when you get into a stressful interaction with the person.

You also may want to practice cueing your deep muscle relaxation in different body positions—sitting, walking, running, and so forth. If you have problems relaxing in certain situations or environments, go back to your original relaxation setting and practice associating relaxation with your relaxation cue (deep breath or the word "relax"). Also, when you are feeling relaxed, imagine yourself in the setting in which you want to use active deep muscle relaxation. If, for example, you get tense and anxious when you have to ride in the back seat of a car, try to imagine yourself in a car while you still are relaxed. If you feel anxiety coming from the imagined situation, practice your cue and then relax away the tension. By practicing with this imagined situation, you can teach yourself to use active deep muscle relaxation in situations that are very difficult for you.

Remember that when you are using this kind of relaxation in specific situations you are not actually tensing and relaxing all your muscle groups. In fact, if you have learned the response well, you probably will not have to use any actual muscle tensing. In essence you can learn to skip the muscle relaxing and get directly to an overall state of relaxation. Do not be concerned if you cannot do this completely. Some people find it helpful and necessary to tense momentarily one or two muscle groups to elicit the relaxation response. In fact for some people tensing and releasing a certain muscle group becomes their cue or signal to relax.

SUMMARY

1. Deep muscle relaxation is a powerful method of relaxation. When your muscles are relaxed deeply, tension and anxiety responses are inhibited.

2. A key ingredient in deep muscle relaxation is the feeling of exaggerated relaxation that comes after you tense a particular muscle group. The feeling allows you to experience deep relaxation and to differentiate it from tension.

3. Deep muscle relaxation can be used as a regular relaxation technique to help reduce your overall tension level.

4. Deep muscle relaxation helps you achieve a state of relaxation that is very similar to meditation (relaxation response). Some people find one technique preferable to the other.

5. In using deep muscle relaxation you need to experiment with the length of time you tense each muscle. The tensing period is usually between 5 and 15 seconds.

6. Deep muscle relaxation will become a kind of conditioned response if you practice it regularly for a few weeks.

7. Practicing on a regular basis is not as easy as it sounds. Remember to find a time and place where you will be uninterrupted and make a strong personal resolution to practice regularly.

8. Deep muscle relaxation also can be used to decrease anxiety in specific situations.

9. This situational use of muscle relaxation is called cue-controlled or *active deep muscle relaxation.*

10. In order to use *active deep muscle relaxation* effectively, you have to be aware of your anxiety and to recognize early signs of tension.

11. You must develop a personal cue or signal to elicit relaxation.

12. This can be developed by pairing a specific cue such as a deep breath or the word "relax" with the general deep muscle relaxation response.

13. Practice active deep muscle relaxation in various settings and body positions so that you can learn to cue-relax in a variety of situations.

SELF-ASSESSMENT
DISCUSSION QUESTIONS

1. What is active deep muscle relaxation? How does it work?

2. Have you ever experienced the kind of profound relaxation described at the beginning of the chapter? Where?

3. How do you first become aware of your anxiety?

4. Do any muscle groups in your body seem to carry most of your tension?

5. Do you have any physical problems that might be related to physical muscle tension (i.e., headaches, stiff neck, backaches, or leg cramps)?

6. Why does deep muscle relaxation inhibit anxiety?

7. Were any of the deep muscle relaxation exercises difficult for you? Why?

8. About how long do you need to tense your muscles in order to produce the desired relaxation feeling?

9. Do you currently use any other kind of technique such as active deep muscle relaxation to cope with particular situations?

10. How would you describe the differences between deep muscle relaxation and meditation? Similarities?

11. Which do you think would work best for you for daily relaxation, meditation or deep muscle relaxation? Why?

ACTIVITIES

Activity 5.1   LEARNING DEEP MUSCLE RELAXATION

Purpose: Help participants learn how to use progressive deep muscle relaxation.

Instructions: Work with a partner and talk each other through the basic deep muscle relaxation exercises. Remember to use a soft voice and to suggest relaxation continually to your partner. Use a cassette tape recorder if you have one available so that each of you will have a tape to use in your individual practice. Discuss your reactions to the experience with your partner and try to answer these questions:

1. Did you experience an overall sense of relaxation?

2. Do you have any problems with particular muscle groups?

3. How did you respond to the other person's voice and delivery?

4. Were you able to differentiate clearly between tension and relaxation?

5. Did you have any other reactions or feelings?

Activity 5.2   DAILY PRACTICE OF DEEP MUSCLE RELAXATION

Purpose: To stimulate regular practice and to highlight beneficial effects.

Instructions: Practice deep muscle relaxation on a daily basis for a week. Find a regular place and time where you will not be disturbed. Keep a log with an entry for each session. Record your reactions, experiences, and any difficulties you have with the technique or with finding time to practice. Look over the log; and if possible, discuss your entries with a partner. What general observations can you make after a week of practice? Did you notice any effects from the exercises on the rest of your life (feeling more relaxed)?

Activity 5.3   ACTIVE DEEP MUSCLE RELAXATION

Purpose: Encourage use and practice of active deep muscle relaxation.

Instructions: Make a list of three or four settings in which you often experience anxiety (i.e., at a lecture, giving a speech, near the telephone, at the breakfast table, in your boss' office). Visit each of these settings and practice active deep muscle relaxation by using a deep breath or the word "relax" as a relaxation cue. (Remember not to attempt active deep muscle relaxation until you have spent a week or two learning the basic deep muscle relaxation technique.) Use active deep muscle relaxation the next time you begin to experience anxiety in each setting. Discuss its effectiveness, problems, success, and needed improvements to make the method work better.

BIBLIOGRAPHY

Ballentine, R. *Science of breath*. Glenville, IL: Himalayan International Institute, 1976.

Deffenbacher, J. L., Michaels, A. C., Michaels, T., & Daley, P. C. Comparison of anxiety management training and self-control desensitization. *Journal of Counseling Psychology*, 1980, *27*, No. 3, 232-239.

Goldfried, M. R. Systematic desensitization as training in self-control. *Journal of Consulting and Clinical Psychology*, 1971, *37*, 228-234.

Goldfried, M. R., & Trier, C. S. Effectiveness of relaxation as an active coping skill. *Journal of Abnormal Psychology*, 1974, *83*, 348-355.

Jacobson, E. *Progressive relaxation*. Chicago: University of Chicago Press, 1938.

Jacobson, E. *Anxiety and tension control: A physiological approach*. Philadelphia: J. B. Lippincott, 1964.

Kanfer, F. H., & Goldstein, A. P. (Eds.). *Helping people change: A textbook of methods*. New York: Pergamon Press, 1975.

Suinn, R., & Richardson, F. Anxiety management training: A non specific therapy program for anxiety control. *Behavior Therapy*, 1971, *4*, 498-510.

Wolpe, J. *The practice of behavior therapy* (2nd ed). New York: Pergamon Press, 1973.

Wolpe, J., & Lazarus, A. A. *Behavior therapy techniques*. New York: Pergamon Press, 1966.

Regular exercise helps combat daily tensions and anxieties.

Chapter 6

NUTRITION
AND EXERCISE

Keeping your body at top operating efficiency is one of the simpliest, yet most difficult ways to manage anxiety. If you take good care of yourself by eating well and exercising, your body and mind will be better able to stand the stresses of daily living. Also, by avoiding some kinds of foods and chemicals you can reduce artificially elevated levels of tension and anxiety.

Although good exercise and nutritional habits improve your general health, the focus of this chapter is on how these practices are related to anxiety management. An understanding of these relationships will help you decide whether your current health habits help or hinder your own management of anxiety. This chapter is not however meant to be another admonition to eat right and get plenty of sleep. Information and suggestions are presented, but you have to decide which ideas make sense for you. Because of the volume of information and theories (many unsubstantiated), a clear understanding of the importance of exercise and nutrition is difficult to attain. One fact does stand out however. General patterns of diet, exercise, and other life style components seem to be related more closely to stress and stress related diseases than most scientists and physicians have assumed previously.

NUTRITION

About the only thing that nutritionists and health experts agree upon with regard to nutrition is that many different opinions prevail. Kenneth

Pelletier (1979, p. 127) said, "No other area of health maintenance is more subject to confusion and misinformation by both laymen and professionals than the role of diet." However, all the experts do agree that complex reactions and interactions in your body clearly are related in some way to what you eat.

Given this complexity, identifying specific dietary practices that are related directly to anxiety is difficult. However, it is not difficult to imagine that the foods and chemicals you consume directly effect your general anxiety level. For example, if you have consumed several cups of coffee, your general state of arousal will be elevated. If you then encounter a difficult situation, your stress reaction may be much greater because you already are somewhat tense. Two things are likely to occur. First, your threshold for stressors will be lower. Events that you normally handle may seem more difficult and therefore cause more tension and anxiety. Second, because you are aroused already, the physical manifestations of stress (muscle tension, heart rate, etc.) will be more pronounced.

You suddenly might find yourself trying to cope with more demands on your time than you feel you can handle. If you are in good shape physically, you probably can summon up the extra energy necessary to handle the situation. If, on the other hand, you have been living on candy bars and junk food and your muscles are atrophied, you probably will not have the necessary energy and clearness of mind.

Four general considerations are significant in examining how you might modify your own nutritional habits: general diet, use of caffeine, use of sugar, and use of vitamins. This list does not exhaust the possible connections between nutrition and stress, but it does provide you with information about the most obvious relationships.

BALANCED DIET

How many times have you heard about the importance of a balanced diet? If you think hard, you can picture your elementary school nurse or health teacher talking about the importance of different food groups. Yet, most health experts tell us that our eating habits have deteriorated significantly over the last several decades. A United States Senate subcommittee (1977) chaired by Senator George McGovern wrote:

The simple fact is that our diets have changed radically within the last 50 years with great and often harmful effects on our health. These dietary changes represent as great a threat to public health as smoking. Too much fat, too much sugar or salt, can be and are linked directly to heart disease, cancer, obesity, and stroke, among other killer diseases. In all six of the ten leading causes of death in the United States have been linked to our diet. (Pelletier, 1979, p. 145)

You do not have to become a vegeterian or begin shopping in health food stores to improve your diet. Although many people are experimenting with radically different kinds of diets, major changes in nutritional habits may not be necessary. You are much more likely to change your eating habits permanently if you make slow progress and if you set realistic goals for yourself.

But what exactly should you do, become a vegeterian, eat a bigger breakfast, fast periodically? Each of these ideas has advocates. Rudolph Ballentine (1979) suggested that because of so much variation in how food affects different people, each person must determine experimentally his/her own optimum diet. He cited an Indian approach to nutrition that categorizes foods into three groups called the three *Gunas. Tasmas* foods are those which are spoiled partly or highly processed. Alcohol and meat (unless it is freshly slaughtered) are considered to be in this category. According to Ballentine (1978), "Such foods *(tasmic)* create a feeling of heaviness, of lethargy: they nourish only the grossest aspects of the body" (p. 547). He cites the following possible behavioral results of *tasmic* food:

—feeling of restlessness and lack of ease
—tyrannical, oppressive kind of disposition
—makes one less alert
—one may vacillate between irascible restlessness and a tendency to fall asleep. (p. 547)

Foods in the second category called *Rajas* usually are highly cooked to increase appeal. They speed up the nervous system and metabolism. These foods include coffee, tea, tobacco, and richly sauced and spiced meat.

Rajasic foods will energize, but not in the sense of lending a clear, balanced energy. Rather, they stimulate and push the

71

organism to increase its speed and to indulge more in physical activity, sensual pleasure, and "creature comforts." (Ballentine, 1978, p. 548)

In describing the third category, *Satlvic* foods, which includes grains and vegetables, Ballentine said that:

By contrast to the above two categories, those foods which are fresh, whole, natural of good quality yet mild, neither over nor undercooked, are experienced as lending a calm alertness and at the same time a state of quiet energy. Such foods are called *Satlvic.* They are said to "nourish the consciousness." They not only provide nourishment for the body, but they do not adversely affect the overall energy state. They add vitality to the total system by bringing a perfect, harmonious balance of energy states in the food itself. They do not *pull* energy from the body, they do not *weigh* it down, they do not *make* it heavier; neither do they irritate it, nor push it beyond its capacity. (Ballentine, 1978, p. 550)

Nutritionists seem to agree that although specifying minimum daily requirements and desired food group balances is possible, the variation among individuals makes general rules difficult. If you would like to experiment with your diet for the specific objective of improving your general health and thereby your ability to cope with stress, do not change your eating habits radically by excluding important nutritional foods. If you do want to make major changes, you should consult literature on nutrition and your physician. If you plan to become a vegeterian, for example, you need to insure that you provide the necessary protein, vitamins, and minerals that you have been getting with meat.

If you want to improve your diet without a radical change in your eating habits, the following suggestions published by the McGovern committee and aimed at the American public may be helpful:

1. Increase consumption of fruits and vegetables and whole grains.

2. Decrease consumption of refined and other processed sugars and foods high in sugars.

3. Decrease consumption of foods high in total fat, and partially replace saturated fats, whether obtained from animal or vegetable sources, with polyunsaturated fats.

4. Decrease consumption of animal fat, and choose meats, poultry, and fish, which reduce saturated fat intake.

5. Except for young children, substitute low-fat and nonfat milk for whole milk, and low-fat dairy products for high fat dairy products.

6. Decrease consumption of butter, fat, eggs, and other high cholesterol sources. Some consideration should be given to easing the cholesterol goal for premenopausal women, young children, and the elderly, in order to obtain the nutritional benefits of eggs in the diet.

7. Decrease consumption of salt and foods high in salt contents. (Bumstead, Field & Carter, 1978, p.116)

SUGAR, CAFFEINE, AND VITAMINS

Sugar

The average American eats about 102 pounds of refined sugar every year—that is a lot of sweetness. Aside from tooth decay and other negative effects, refined sugars can effect your stress level directly. Because refined sugar is absorbed quickly into the bloodstream, one frequently experiences a quick spurt of energy. Problems often occur when no real physical work uses up the energy and it becomes *nervous* energy and may be experienced as a vague sense of anxiety. Physiological components of this "sugar energy" are similar to those of the stress or "fight and flight" response. The end result is an increased arousal state. As part of the body's response, the pancreas produces insulin to counteract the sugar. Sometimes an overabundance of insulin is produced and the individual feels lethargic and slightly depressed. To counter this feeling many people will then reach for another candy bar or cup of sugared tea or coffee. The see-saw effect of these ups and downs can have negative psychological effects. One result of the constant activity of the pancreas in attempting to counterbalance excessive sugar is hypoglycemia. This condition, which can have emotional side effects, may lead to further and more serious insulin imbalance problems like diabetes. Although the over consumption of refined sugar does not necessarily cause these problems, the body's mechanisms for using sugar can be strained by the very large amounts of sugar that are consumed.

73

Another problem with too much sugar consumption is the percentage of calories that it provides. Because sugar calories are empty (they do not provide other needed nutrients and chemicals), they should not be used in place of protein, which supplies other necessary substances, and also releases sugar more slowly into the bloodstream. The McGovern committee's dietary goals for the United States suggested about a 45 percent reduction of refined and processed sugar (Bumstead, Field, & Carter, 1978)

Caffeine

Caffeine is another villain. Everyone knows that caffeine is a stimulant and that too much caffeine can cause tension and nervousness. But even with this knowledge too few people actually monitor their caffeine intake. The overuse of caffeine is similar to the overuse of sugar in many respects. By stimulating the body, biochemical reactions are produced that increase the general arousal level and often cause *free floating* anxiety. Caffeine is contained in coffee, cola, tea, pain medications (such as Empirin), and cocoa (chocolate).

What is too much caffeine? This determination will vary from person to person. Some people may react negatively to just one cup of coffee while others can tolerate several cups. Certainly, if the equivalent of three or four cups of coffee or strong tea a day is exceeded, one needs to take a look at his/her own consumption habits. Remember also that coffee and sugars interact. One very easily can get on the up and down cycle described for sugar abusers by using coffee and sugar. If an individual is a caffeine or sugar addict, he/she is producing excess energy, free floating anxiety, and paradoxically also creating periods of lethargy and depression that he/she may become compelled to counteract with a dose of sugar or caffeine or both.

Decreasing your refined sugar and caffeine intake is in your best interest. But how? Anyone who has ever walked down a supermarket cereal aisle with a child can attest to the strong cultural influences on children and adults to over consume sugar. A good way to start controlling your intake of refined sugars and caffeine is to keep track of how much you do consume. This kind of charting will help you assess your intake and may give you some idea of the relationship between your use of sugar and caffeine and your feelings of anxiety. You can use a variety of recording methods. The easiest method is to record in a small notebook at each consumption. If you do not want to go to that much trouble, at the end of each day write amounts and times you have had sugar or caffeine. The times are important because they help you become aware of patterns and also link consumption to your mood. This assessment process in itself may help you better control your intake of these substances.

After you have taken a hard look at your own habits, you may want to decrease sugar and caffeine. From the standpoint of anxiety management, you may not be able to determine the effects of caffeine and sugars until you experiment with reducing or eliminating them. There are two relatively simple ways to decrease your use of these substances.

Substitution. One way to use less sugar and caffeine is to substitute another but similar substance. You can, for example, use artifical sweetners, or decaffinated coffee. Or you can substitute hot bouillon or weak or herbal tea for coffee. When you get the urge to eat something sweet, you can substitute carrot sticks, celery, or some other healthier food. You may want to practice what behavioral psychologists call *stimulus control*—in more common language, do not keep the stuff around the house. Or at least, do not keep it out where you will be tempted all the time. A plate of cookies, a box of candy, or a perking coffee pot are temptations that are hard to combat. If you plan to use artificial sweetners, or decaffinated coffee investigate the latest reports on potentially dangerous effects of these substances.

Reduction. Reducing your intake of caffeine and sugar is easier than totally eliminating them. Most individuals will not give up that morning cup of coffee or an occasional desert. However giving up the second cup of coffee or allowing yourself something really sweet less frequently is less difficult. Reduce the amount of coffee that you make at home, or turn your coffee cup over when you are out to let the waitress or waiter know that you do not want an additional cup. A reasonable goal for most Americans would be to reduce their intake of refined sugars and caffeine by 40 to 50 percent. Experiment yourself with your caffeine intake, at least long enough to determine if you do feel better and less anxious.

Vitamins

A number of claims have been made that Vitamin C and B complex vitamins are related to stress (Mason, 1980; Ballentine, 1978). Ballentine in his book, *Diet and Nutrition,* concluded the following:

In summary, then, it appears that we can conclude that the more chronically anxious person who tends to interpret events around him as disturbing will, as a result of the more frequent occurrences of those metabolic events that accompany his tense and anxious behavior, use up more of certain nutrients which are involved in his characteristic responses. It will generally be some combination of certain of the B vitamins and/or vitamin C* which are required in the most unusual quantities by those who tend to respond psychologically and physiologically with "anxiety." But there is no set proportion of B vitamins and C that is needed by every "stressed" person. (Ballentine, 1978, p. 522)

As in many nutrition related questions no definitive answers have been formulated. Apparently, some vitamin B complex and C vitamins are depleted more rapidly by stress reactions. If this conclusion is true, people who are under stress should supplement their diet with B complex and C vitamins. Part of the negative physical effect of stress reactions can be mediated and the body may more easily cope with additional anxiety. According to Pelletier (1979) there are few toxic effects associated with Vitamins B and C. He lists possible negative side effects for more than 100 mg daily of Vitamin B—Niacin, and diuretic and laxative effects of excessive Vitamin C for some people. He also mentions an unproven association between excessive Vitamin C and kidney stones for some people.

Supplements of C and B vitamins are available in most drug and health food stores. In general, taking supplementary vitamins and chemicals should be approached with caution. Also, remember to consider cost-benefit questions. It may be better from a stress management perspective to put the money you spend on vitamins into a pair of good running shoes or toward the purchase of copies of your resume to help you get a less-stress-producing job.

DRUGS AND ANXIETY

In our culture drugs are used to help decrease feelings of anxiety. Tranquilizers like valium and librium continue to be the most widely prescribed drugs in the United States. Alcohol and marijuana are used

---

*The "stress tabs" now sold in many health food stores contain the vitamin B complex plus vitamin C with higher quantities of pantothenic acid which is thought to help the adrenals.

widely as "recreation drugs" that are consumed very often in order to help a person feel calmer. Because of the widespread use and availability of these drugs, one is almost assured of being faced with a decision about their use. Tranquilizers differ from marijuana and alcohol in that they are prescription drugs used specifically for anxiety reactions. Alcohol and marijuana often are used to alleviate tension; however they also are used for other recreational purposes and are part of various cultural events and traditions.

Are these drugs harmful, or do they offer an easy and harmless way to relax? Alcohol and marijuana can have negative side effects, particularly when used frequently and with high dosage. Alcoholism is a major problem in our culture and causes millions of people psychological and physical suffering. In the extreme, people can die from alcohol poisoning. However, millions of people also use alcohol in moderation with no apparent negative effects. Two problems can occur from using alcohol as a relaxor. First, if one is prone to alcoholism or alcohol abuse, it is easy to gradually increase dosage until a serious drinking problem results. Second, if alcohol is used to relax, individuals are relying on an external substance to help them cope and probably are not developing natural coping anxiety management skills.

In the last decade or two, marijuana has become the drug of choice for many people. Considerable controversy as to the ill effects of marijuana still exists. Recent research seems to indicate that it is not a harmless substance and that it can have harmful effects, particularly on adolescents who are not finished growing physically. Heavy use of marijuana also frequently produces what has been called the "amotivational syndrome." Some users become apathetic and unable to accept and meet life's challenges. In this case they have managed their anxiety so much that they stop the growth and development that comes from the positive challenges related to anxiety.

Tranquilizers, when used judiciously, appear to have few negative effects. The major problem seems to develop from dependence by people who use them too frequently. After a while these people are unable to cope with any stress without their pills. Historically, many physicians have over prescribed tranquilizers. These drugs do have a role in anxiety management when they are used sparingly after an adequate diagnosis. They can help people get through difficult crisis situations without losing all of their other coping mechanisms.

77

In general, none of these drugs provides an adequate long-term mechanism for managing anxiety. Other relaxation techniques such as those covered in this book can provide similar physical relaxation without the danger of side effects or the necessity of putting unnecessary chemicals in your body.

EXERCISE

It is not possible to drive down the road these days without seeing people jogging. They often have pained expressions on their faces, and look as if they are about to expire, yet they keep on going. Why? Because in the long run they feel better. If you have ever been in excellent physical condition, you will recognize that feeling of stamina and well being that exercise enthusiasts readily describe.

Regular exercise can help you with anxiety management in several ways. During vigorous exercise you get a respite from your daily worries and concerns. For at least 20 or 30 minutes all you concentrate on is running, swimming, or whatever exercise you choose. The pent-up tension that you have not been able to express physically can be released, and the regular use of various muscle groups conditions your body so that stress responses can be tolerated better.

In addition to these direct physical benefits there are a number of psychological ones. Generally you look better and perform better with both your body and mind operating more efficiently. Your sense of self-confidence and self-worth often improves, and you are better able to manage difficult situations. The sense of self-control that comes with being in tune with your physical being is both calming and energizing.

Types of Exercises

Before discussing how you can develop your own exercise program it may be helpful to identify different types of exercises. Generally speaking there are two categories of exercises—those that build strength and improve muscle tone and those that build over-all endurance. Exercises like weight training, calisthenics, and isometrics are primarily used to build muscle and improve appearance and strength. Exercises like running, walking, swimming, and cycling are more often used to build endurance. These endurance building exercises are called aerobic exercises. Of course, these categories are not discrete. Swimming, for example, helps you build strength and improve your appearance as well as increasing your endurance.

Aerobic exercises are generally more helpful for anxiety management because of their overall positive effect on the cardiovascular system. In essence your heart is trained to operate more efficiently and, therefore beat less frequently during normal resting periods. Dr. Kenneth Cooper (1976) first brought this notion of a training effect to the attention of the general public. He outlines the importance of aerobic exercises very persuasively in several books. (Cooper, 1975, 1976, 1977).

Choosing an Exercise Program

There are, of course, a number of already designed exercise programs available. The Royal Canadian Exercise Program (5BX) (Duhamel, 1962) which includes endurance and strength building exercises is available for men and women. Like most organized programs this one starts you out slowly and you work up to a certain level according to your age. There are several charts and levels within charts, and each session takes about 20 minutes. Dr. Cooper, in *The Aerobics Way*, (1977) also provides a variety of charts and an aerobic point system to help you design a program. Dr. Cooper's approach allows you more flexibility because he provides charts for a great variety of exercises (walking/running, cycling, swimming, handball/racquetball/squash, and stationary cycling).

Some people find it helpful to join a health spa or gymnasium. Although these facilities sometimes are expensive, they can make exercising more enjoyable. The fancier spas have numerous steam and sauna baths and relaxing whirlpools. If you choose this kind of program remember that the requirement is for some kind of sustained exercise to produce the training effect. Because many people going to spas are concerned more with their physical appearance, the trainer may not emphasize aerobic exercises. If a spa does not appeal to you, consider something like aerobic dancing. Classes usually meet several times a week and provide the training effect by engaging you in vigorous dance activity. These classes frequently are offered at local colleges and YWCA's.

Perhaps you do not like regimented programs? Then make up your own! You may need some kind of written plan, though, particularly if you are starting at a low level of fitness. The key is gradual increases and consistency in whatever exercise you choose. Remember also to be certain that no medical problems exist that would make vigorous exercise dangerous for you. If you have not had a physical recently, you should check with your doctor before you start on any program.

79

The key to success is finding something that you will enjoy and continue to perform. It may take some experimentation before you find just the right kind of exercise for yourself. You must, of course, start out slowly no matter what you choose. Too many people plunge into exercise programs without careful enough planning and wind up miserable after two days with a perfect excuse for quitting. Some hints about how to stay motivated will be presented later.

Equipment, Clothes, and Weather

Part of the fun of exercise can be obtaining the equipment. You really do not need designer running pants to jog; but good shoes, appropriate clothes and equipment are important. Talking with someone in a reputable sporting goods store, or better yet, a physical education instructor is a good idea. Loose fitting clothing for jogging is advised in accordance with weather conditions. During lower temperatures remember to cover your head and hands. If you plan to jog, do not put on just any old pair of tennis shoes—jogging jars your whole body and you need the best support and cushioning effect that you can get.

Exercising in hot weather presents more potential difficulties than in cold weather. The primary danger is overheating and dehydration. Your body increases its overall temperature when you exercise, and in very hot and humid weather your natural cooling system does not work as well. In hot weather try to exercise in the cooler parts of the day, drink plenty of fluids, and reduce the intensity of your exercise. In cold weather remember that exercise will increase your temperature. If outdoors, dress in layers so that you can unzip or remove excess clothing if necessary. In windy, cold weather, beware of frost bite and windburn. If you live in a high air pollution area, you may want to restrict your activity when the pollution index reaches the warning levels.

Warm-up/Cool-down

According to Pollack, Wilmore, and Fox III (1978), including a warm-up procedure in an endurance exercise program is essential. If you are following a particular program, like 5BX, a warm-up is built into the program. If you are on your own, you need to include stretching exercises to prepare muscles, ligaments, and joints for vigorous exercise. A cool-down period of five to ten minutes also is essential to help the leg muscles return blood to the heart, i.e., in activities such as jogging. According to Pollack et al. "Without the light activity, the blood will con-

80

tinue to pool in the lower body, and the participant may experience dizziness and can even pass out because of inadequate blood flow to the
brain" (1978, p. 233).

Medical Considerations

In the following circumstances you should stop exercising and see a
physician before resuming.

1. Abnormal heart activity, including irregular pulse (missed
beats or extra beats), fluttering, jumping or palpitations in the
chest or throat, sudden burst of rapid heart beats, or a sudden
slowing of a rapid pulse rate.

2. Pain or pressure in the center of the chest, or the arm or
throat, during or immediately following exercise.

3. Dizziness, lightheadedness, sudden lack of coordination, confusion, cold sweating, glassy stare, pallor, blueness or fainting.

4. Illness, particularly viral infections, can lead to myocarditis,
that is, viral infection of the heart muscle. Avoid exercise during
and immediately following an illness. (Pollack et al., 1978, p.
234)

In these situations you can attempt the following self-corrections.

1. Persistent rapid pulse rate throughout 5 to 10 minutes of
recovery or longer.

Self-correction technique: reduce intensity of the activity (use a lower training heart rate) and progress to
higher levels of activity at a slower rate. Consult a physician if the condition persists.

2. Nausea or vomiting after exercise.

Self-correction technique: reduce the intensity of the
endurance exercise and prolong the cool down period.
Avoid eating for at least two hours prior to the exercise
session.

81

3. Extreme breathlessness lasting more than 10 minutes after the cessation of exercise.

Self-correction technique: reduce the intensity of the endurance exercise. Consult a physician if the condition persists.

4. Prolonged fatigue up to 24 hours following exercise.

Self-correction technique: reduce the intensity of the endurance exercise and reduce the duration of the total workout session if this symptom persists. Consult a physician if these self-correction techniques do not remedy the situation. (Pollack et al., 1978, p.234)

Motivation

Regular exercise is beneficial physically and psychologically, yet most individuals do not follow a consistent program. It takes time and the beginning weeks while one is working up to a tolerable endurance level can be difficult and discouraging.

Perhaps the first step is to make a real decision that you want to exercise. Half-hearted attempts are bound to fail, as are unrealistic approaches. Do something that makes sense for you. If you are definitely not a morning person, then do not decide to get up an hour early to exercise. Making radical changes in your habits and life style is not impossible, but success is more likely if you use what you know about yourself. If you are married or a family member, discuss your plans with the people who live with you so that your schedule will be compatible with their schedules. If social reinforcement helps you, and it does most people, try to get some friends involved with you. The obligation to be out to meet a friend might make the difference for you on days when you want to quit; or join a class, spa, or some other organized activity. Even if the program costs you, it will be worthwhile if you develop a sustained exercise program.

Keep track of your progress. If you keep track of miles run, pounds lost, heart rate, and so forth, you will have something tangible to keep you going. Consider making a chart or some kind of record. Also, notice how you feel. Keep a record of the differences in energy level, sense of relaxation, sleep patterns, sex patterns, etc. The more you realize the positive effects, the better motivated you will become.

Use behavior modification techniques on yourself. Reward yourself if you exercise regularly. Keep your exercise equipment where you will see it frequently to remind you to use it. For example, you can put your running shoes by the front door on days that you plan to run. Condition yourself to exercise at a regular time and place. Try to make exercise become automatic.

Expect failures and frustrations, but do not use your failures as excuses to give up. If you miss exercising for a week, you may be tempted to give up, feeling that you have lost the training effect. Do not. You always regain the training effect and you may be amazed at how much endurance you have retained. Allow yourself some days off. At times you just will not feel like vigorous exercise. As long as these days do not occur regularly, it is okay to skip exercising occasionally. Beware of the trap, though, where you begin to rationalize frequent variations from your schedule. Regularity is the most important key to success.

SUMMARY

1. If your body is generally in good shape, you will be able to manage stress better.

2. An understanding of the relationship among nutrition, exercise, and health can help you decide how your diet and exercise habits effect your stress levels.

3. Although there is considerable controversy about the effects of what we eat, complex reactions and interrelationships do exist between diet and behavior.

4. Foods and chemical substances can effect your general level of physical arousal and therefore your threshold for tension and anxiety.

5. A balanced diet can help to provide the physical and mental mechanisms necessary to cope with anxiety.

6. American dietary habits generally are poor. Individuals eat too much salt, sugar, and animal fat.

7. Improving your diet can be done most easily with gradual changes.

8. Because individual nutrition needs vary, depending upon any prescribed pattern is difficult.

9. One approach to nutrition is to view foods in groups and to insure an adequate amount of food from each group is eaten.

10. An Indian approach divides foods into three *Gunas* with specific feelings and attitudes identified for each group.

11. The McGovern Committee examined nutrition in America and suggested the following general changes:

a. more fruits, vegetables, and whole grains
b. decreased refined sugar and high sugar foods
c. decreased fats and higher percentage of unsaturated fats
d. decreased animal fats (meat) and increased fish and poultry
e. low-fat and non-fat milk
f. decreased butter fat, eggs, and high cholesterol items
g. decreased salt

12. Excessive use of sugar can produce anxiety by providing too much quick energy which if not used results in up periods of stimulation and down periods of fatigue and depression.

13. Caffeine in excess also can produce tension and anxiety.

14. Use of caffeine and sugar can be reduced to acceptable levels by reduction and substitution.

15. A and B complex vitamins are used up quickly during periods of tension and anxiety. Supplements are obtainable easily and appear to have no serious side effects.

16. Various drugs like alcohol, marijuana, and tranquilizers can be used to decrease anxiety, but they generally are not effectve long-term solutions.

17. Regular exercise can improve anxiety management abilities in several ways:

a. as a diversion,
b. physical expression of tension,
c. improved sense of well being,
d. increased physical ability to tolerate stress, and
e. generally improved performance.

18. Aerobic exercises, by which you achieve a "training effect" by sustaining activity over 10 to 20 minutes, probably are most helpful.

19. Three approaches to exercising can be useful:

a. following a specific program (such as 5BX, or aerobic points)
b. joining a class, spa, or organized group, or
c. developing your own program.

20. Any approach should be gradual with medical support and approval.

21. Novice exercisers need to gather information about special clothing, equipment, and about various weather conditions.

22. A warm-up period including stretching exercises and a brief cooldown period are necessary.

23. Any unusual heart activity, dizziness, chest pressure, illness, or other medical problems should be taken seriously and checked before the resumption of exercise.

24. Motivation is the key factor in developing a sustained exercise program. Spend time thinking about how to keep yourself motivated and then build in as many positive motivation factors as possible.

SELF-ASSESSMENT
DISCUSSION QUESTIONS

1. Do you agree with the hypothesis that the general state of your health is related to tension and anxiety levels?

2. How do your nutritional habits effect your tension and anxiety levels?

3. How would you rate the quality of your diet?

4. Have you ever experimented with different dietary practices e.g., vegeterian, special diets, etc.? Did it seem to effect your anxiety levels?

5. How do sugar and caffeine effect anxiety?

6. What is meant by the sugar/coffee up and down cycle?

85

7. Are you familiar with the sugar content of the foods you eat?

8. How would you rate the amount of sugar and caffeine that you use?

9. List some ways that one can substitute or reduce caffeine and sugar intake.

10. Why are vitamins C and B complex sometimes called "stress vitamins"?

11. Do you believe that alcohol, marijuana, and tranquilizers are useful relaxation drugs?

12. How does regular exercise help in anxiety management?

13. What is your attitude toward exercise?

14. What is meant by the training effect?

15. What factors are important in choosing an exercise?

16. Why is gradual conditioning important?

17. How can exercising in hot weather be dangerous?

18. What is the purpose of the cool-down period?

19. What type of exercise program would be most suitable for you?

20. List some ways to create and maintain motivation for exercising.

21. What would be your greatest difficulties in developing and practicing a sustained exercise program?

ACTIVITIES

Activity 6.1 DIET ANALYSIS

Purpose: To increase awareness of personal dietary habits.

Instructions: For the next three or four days keep a detailed record of what you eat. Using the three *Gunas* system or a more traditional system analyze your nutritional habits. Is your diet balanced? Was this a typical three day period? List several changes that are necessary to bring your diet more into balance. Discuss your plans with your work group or with a friend.

Activity 6.2 SUGAR AND CAFFEINE USE

Purpose: Explore the relationship between anxiety and the use of sugar and caffeine.

Instructions: Record your use of sugar and caffeine for three days. Remember to include foods high in sugar. Record your mood as you use the sugar or caffeine, 15 minutes after use, and two hours after use. Look for patterns and reactions specifically focusing on anxiety. Do you experience the up and down cycle? Discuss you findings with your work group or a friend.

Activity 6.3 PERSONAL EXERCISE PLAN

Purpose: Encourage development of an exercise plan and increase awareness of the relationship between exercise and anxiety.

Instructions: Develop an exercise plan for yourself and try it out for one week. If necessary clear it with your physician. Each time you exercise, record your general mood and energy level one hour after you exercise, three hours after you exercise, and six hours after you exercise. Also, each morning when you get up, record your general mood and energy level and make a notation of how well you slept. You may need to consult one of Cooper's books or other sources to plan your program. Discuss your plan and its effect on you with your work group or a friend.

Activity 6.4 MOTIVATION AND BLOCKS TO EXERCISE

Purpose: To explore ways to develop and sustain an effective exercise program.

Instructions: List at least four ways that you can keep yourself motivated to continue exercising. Also list at least four blocks to exercising that you can anticipate and strategies to overcome these blocks. Seek suggestions from your work group or friends.

BIBLIOGRAPHY

Albright, E. P., & Albright, P. *Body, mind and spirit: The journey toward health and wholeness.* Brattlebord, Vermont: The Stephen Greene Press, 1980.

Ballentine, R. *Diet and nutrition: A holistic approach.* Honesdale, Pennsylvania: The Himalayan International Institute, 1978. Address: RD1, Box 88, Honesdale, PA 18431

Bumstead, C., Field, A., & Carter, B. *Nutrition: How much can government help?* Washington D.C.: Concern, Inc., 2233 Wisconsin Avenue, N.W., Washington, D.C., 1978.

Burton, B. T. *Human nutrition* (3rd ed.). Formerly the *Heinz handbook of nutrition*. New York: McGraw-Hill, 1976.

Clark, L. *The new way to eat*. Millbrae, California: Celestial Arts, 1980.

Cooper, K. H. *The new aerobics*. New York: Bantam Books, 1975.

Cooper, K. H. *Aerobics*. New York: Bantam Books, 1976.

Cooper, K. H. *The aerobics way*. New York: M. Evans & Co., 1977.

Dietary goals for the United States. A report of the select committee on nutrition and human needs. (2nd ed.). G. McGovern, chairperson, U. S. Senate, Washington, D. C., 1977, Stock Number 052-070-04376-8.

Dietary goals for the United States--supplemental views. Select Committee on Nutrition and Human Needs. G. McGovern, chairperson, U. S. Senate, Washington, D. C.

Duhamel, R. *Royal Canadian Air Force exercise plans for physical fitness.* Canada: Essandess, 1962.

Falls, H. B., Wallis, E. L., & Logan, G. A. *Foundations of conditioning.* New York: Academic Press, 1970.

Glasser, W. *Positive addiction*. New York: Harper and Row, 1976.

Mackey, R. T. *Exercise rest and relaxation*. Dubuque, Iowa: William C. Brown Co., 1970.

Mason, L. J. *Guide to stress reduction*. Culver City, California: Peace Press, 1980.

Pelletier, K. R. (Ed.). *Holistic medicine: From stress to optimum health.* New York: Delacorte Press, 1979.

Pollack, M. L., Wilmore, J. H., & Fox III, S. M. *Health and fitness through physical activity.* New York: John Wiley and Sons, 1978.

Rodale, J. I. *The complete book of vitamins*. Emmaus, Pennsylvania: Rodale Press, 1977.

Williams, R. J. *Biochemical individuality: The basis for the genetotrophic concept.* New York: John Wiley and Sons, 1956.

Williams, R. J. *The wonderful world within you: Your nutritional environment.* New York: Bantam Books, 1977.

Williams, R. J., & Kalita, D. K. *A physicians handbook on orthomolecular medicine.* New York: Pergamon Press, 1977.

PART III

COGNITIVE APPROACHES: BELIEFS AND SELF-STATEMENTS

Part III

COGNITIVE APPROACHES: BELIEFS AND SELF-STATEMENTS

In this section you will explore the relationship between anxiety and your thought processes. In particular you will see how worrysome and irrational beliefs can produce unnecessary and frequently harmful anxiety. In Chapter 7 you will examine the relationships between your belief system and anxiety. Albert Ellis's (1962) system of Rational-Emotive psychotherapy will be described with particular emphasis on anxiety and anxiety management.

In Chapter 8 you will learn how the statements that you make to yourself affect your anxiety level and performance in various situations. Meichenbaum's (1977, 1979) stress inoculation procedure will be introduced as a way to modify situational anxiety positively. Because this method also involves deep muscle relaxation, you will dicover how physical and cognitive approaches can be combined to help fight excessive anxiety.

Chapter 7

IRRATIONAL THINKING AND ANXIETY

"Men are disturbed not by things, but by the view they take of them." This quotation by Epictetus, a Roman Stoic philosopher, often appears in Albert Ellis' (1977) descriptions of his Rational Emotive approach to psychotherapy. The quotation is also a good introduction to this chapter because it suggests the importance of thinking and self-statements in the anxiety process. What you say to yourself about an anxiety provoking situation can create or greatly increase your anxiety. For example, if you are worried and anxious about a job interview, what you are thinking and saying to yourself about that situation can cause anxiety. You might say something such as, "I am really nervous, I know I am going to mess up this interview." According to Ellis this negative self-statement and its basic belief causes anxiety, not the interview itself. You will learn more about this kind of negative self-statement and related underlying beliefs later in this chapter.

MIND APPROACH VERSUS BODY APPROACH

Because this cognitive (mind) approach is so different from the body-oriented (physical) anxiety management methods that you previously learned, discussing the differences may be helpful. You will recall that the body-oriented methods focus on helping people achieve deeper relaxation states. In a sense in these methods the assumption is that if you reduce the physical manifestations of anxiety you will experience an overall decrease in anxiety. The cognitive approach focuses instead on how the mind creates anxiety. In a sense this difference is a chicken and egg question. Does anxiety in your body come as a result of your thinking, or do you feel anxiety and then think about it? Although the two approaches may seem contradictory they can be used to complement each other. In fact, by learning to modify your thinking and your body responses you can develop a doubly potent way of managing anxiety.

IRRATIONAL BELIEFS

Ellis (1977) believes that because people have irrational beliefs they often make irrational statements to themselves when they are interpreting life events and situations. But why are individuals so frequently irrational in their beliefs? According to Ellis (1962, 1977) western society and its institutions have taught individuals to place too much emphasis on guilt, obligation, and achievement. Ellis believes that many of the values of our competitive society are self-defeating. Ellis (1962, 1977) listed eleven *irrational* beliefs that are common to western man:

1. It is a dire necessity for an adult human being to be loved or approved by virtually every other significant person in his/her community. (Ellis, 1962, p. 61)

This belief is very common. Many people feel that they must have other people's approval in order to be worthwhile. In the extreme, this belief can cause a person to be on edge constantly, always worrying about how his/her every word or behavior affects others. Many people who hold this belief probably learned as young children that pleasing others was an absolute necessity.

2. One should be thoroughly competent, adequate, and achieving in all possible respects if one is to consider oneself worthwhile. (Ellis, 1962, p. 63)

This belief is clearly in tune with our achievement-oriented culture. Most of us learn early that competence and achievement bring big rewards. The problem comes when individuals set up an equation where very high achievement is necessary to be a worthwhile human being. Persons become so demanding of themselves that adequate levels of achievement are never really reached. Therefore, they are never really satisfied with themselves.

3. Certain people are bad, wicked, villainous, and they should be severely blamed and punished for their villainy. (Ellis, 1962, p. 65)

This belief is applied in two ways. People use it on themselves: that is, they believe they are basically bad and deserve punishment. Or, the belief can be used with respect to others. In both cases it tends to produce fear, anxiety, and guilt.

4. It is awful and catastrophic when things are not the way one would very much like them to be. (Ellis, 1962, p. 69)

Everyone loses his/her perspective at times and believes that some event or situation is an absolute catastrophe. If this belief becomes a dominant one for an individual, he/she will go through life constantly facing crises. These crises are, of course, because of the belief and expectation that things should always be orderly and predictable. Life just does not work that way.

5. Human unhappiness is externally caused and individuals have little or no ability to control their sorrows and disturbances. (Ellis, 1962, p. 72)

Externalizing troubles is simple because it's so much easier to blame other people or things and thereby avoid responsibility for one's own behavior. Certainly uncontrollable external events do impact our lives, but a belief that external events actually can control us robs us of much of our power and humanity. People who believe that they always are acted upon are seldom at ease, because they never really know from where the next threat will come.

6. If something is or may be dangerous or fearsome, one should be terribly concerned about it and should keep dwelling on the possibility of its occurring. (Ellis, 1962, p. 75)

Personification of this belief is the overprotective mother who is worried constantly about something happening to her son or daughter. Life is full of dangers that have to be avoided at all costs. To understand how this kind of belief system can limit a person's life and create a constant edge of anxiety is easy. Even if life carries considerable danger at times, being overzealous in one's fear of danger is not helpful. The young man who is overprotected greatly by his mother is apt to grow up taking very few risks and probably miss much of the texture and richness of life.

7. It is easier to avoid than to face certain difficulties and self-responsibilities. (Ellis, 1972, p. 78)

Everyone has experienced the kind of push-pull feeling that comes from approaching and then avoiding a difficult task or responsibility. The "if you ignore it long enough it will go away" philosophy sometimes works, but more frequently it creates anxiety and ultimately self-deprivation.

8. One should be dependent on others and need someone stronger than oneself on whom to rely. (Ellis, 1962, p. 80)

In the past, women particularly have been prone to this irrational belief. This myth is not surprising because until recently the idea that a woman "needed" a man was prevalent in this society. However, many men also believe that they need someone to take care of them. Accompanying this belief is another irrational belief that the individual in "need" is weak and not capable of caring for him/herself. The opposite of this belief, that one should be totally independent and never dependent on others is equally irrational. Times occur frequently when it is appropriate to be dependent and to be taken care of; however, this need is healthy only within the context of a relationship that is reciprocal.

9. One's past history is an all-important determiner of one's present behavior, and because something once strongly affected one's life, it should have a similar effect indefinitely. (Ellis, 1962, p. 82)

Sometimes people believe they are scarred for life because of childhood experiences or deprivations. Certainly one's background and past experiences influence development, but the past really does not determine what happens in the present or future. This belief often is part of a defense system that protects a person from the risk of trying new behavior or a new way of living.

10. One should become quite upset over other people's problems and disturbances. (Ellis, 1962, p. 85)

Not becoming emotionally touched by the problems and difficulties facing people one knows and cares about is difficult. However, if an individual takes on the problems and difficulties of the world, he/she is apt to spend nearly every waking hour worrying about somebody or something. This irrational belief is hazardous particularly for practitioners in helping professions. If a counselor, physician, or teacher takes on the problems of those with whom he/she is working, his/her effectiveness as a professional soon is diminished. In a sense, this same dynamic works between people in general. If you lose your sense of objectivity and perspective concerning other people's problems, you are less likely to be able to offer help and support.

11. There is invariably a right, precise, and perfect solution to human problems and it is catastrophic if this perfect solution to human problems is not found. (Ellis, 1962, pp. 86-87)

Everyone knows at least one perfectionist—perhaps you are one yourself. Some people are even proud of needing perfection, to the point where they will sometimes boast about it. Unfortunately, the need to be perfect carries with it an incredible amount of pressure and anxiety. Many people confuse the desirability of working toward higher levels of competence with the necessity of things being exactly right. A dangerous side effect of this perfectionistic belief is the underlying assumption that one must achieve perfection in order to be a productive and worthwhile person. The person who needs perfection could be visualized as someone running on a treadmill that constantly increases its speed so that the person never reaches his/her destination. After all, how many perfect people are in this world?

YOUR OWN
IRRATIONAL BELIEFS

You need a reasonably good understanding of your own irrational beliefs. Nearly everyone has irrational beliefs at one time or another. Read the list of eleven beliefs again and try to determine the ones that you use most often. Remember that your words may be different, therefore, you may have to do some translating. You may find it helpful to try to figure out how you came to believe the irrational beliefs that you hold. For example, if you are very achievement oriented and tend to believe that you have to be extremely competent to be worthwhile, you might think back to your school days and ask yourself how you, as a child or young adult, concluded that you had to be highly competent to be worthwhile. Your parents, of course, probably were strong influences as were your peers and your cultural/social environment. Perhaps your father/mother did not have a chance to complete school and was therefore always very insistent about your doing well in school. As a result of this parental value, you may have concluded, probably incorrectly, that you had to achieve at very high levels in order to please your father/mother.

The adult version of this belief is irrational statement number two which states that one has to be *thoroughly* competent. Understanding how you developed this belief will not magically help you become more rational, but the insight and understanding may assist you in giving up an essentially harmful and irrational belief.

CHANGING YOUR
IRRATIONAL BELIEFS

As you read over Ellis's (1962) list of common irrational beliefs you were probably impressed by the obvious irrationality of some, and puzzled by the seeming rationality of others. In order to use this particular method to manage anxiety, you will learn why each of these statements is, indeed, irrational. This learning will have to be personal—that is you will have to understand how your own irrational beliefs are irrational.

This may not be as easy as you imagine. First, you have to be able to identify specific irrational beliefs. This identification can be tricky because irrational beliefs frequently have been part of an individual's belief system since childhood. Also, although some irrational beliefs cause considerable anxiety, they may be highly rewarded by parents and peers. Belief number eight, for example, states that one should be dependent on others and need someone stronger than oneself on whom to rely. This role is clearly the one that some women learn from parents and society. Understanding and accepting the irrationality of this statement may require much personal strength and fortitude.

Of course understanding and identifying are only the beginning steps. You have to be able to modify your irrational beliefs in order to manage your anxiety successfully. A four-step process is necessary: (1) identify, (2) challenge, (3) modify, and (4) practice. Modification is probably most easily done by analyzing individual anxiety situations and the roles of irrational statements and thinking. Ellis (1962) uses what he calls the ABC method for this process. Much of the balance of this chapter will involve learning the ABC method.

By evaluating your general belief system you can get a good idea of which irrational beliefs you are most likely to use in various anxiety situations. You may recognize, for example, that you are a perfectionist and that Irrational Belief number eleven is one that you are likely to use.

THE ABC METHOD

Using the ABC method (Ellis, 1962) involves sorting out several different parts of an anxiety reaction. Ellis (1962) suggests using this method to deal with a wide range of emotional and behavioral problems. The examples and applications, however, will concern only the applications in managing anxiety.

In applying the ABC method to anxiety management use the following definitions:

A—the event or situation that precipitates anxiety feelings

B—beliefs and self-statements about the situations

C—anxiety and negative behaviors

Remember, also, that the situation or event is not always simple or distinct. Two examples follow to illustrate how this ABC system works.

Example 1. *Tom is going to attend a party where he doesn't know anyone (A—situation/event). On the way to the party he feels very anxious and when he gets to the party he goes directly to the bar, gets drunk, and stumbles out without really talking with anyone (C—anxiety feelings and negative behaviors).*

Example 2. *Sharon is becoming less productive on her job. The quality and quantity of her work has been decreasing slowly for several weeks (A—situation/event in this case evolves over a period of time). She has a vague sense of anxiety, dissatisfaction and her absences from work are increasing (C—negative feelings and behaviors).*

101

In both of these examples you might be tempted to say that (A), the situation, caused (C), the negative feelings and behaviors. *Not so!* You have to add another step, (B), which identifies a person's *beliefs* and *self-statements* about the situation, (A). In other words, the meaning or interpretation that one places on the event is the crucial variable.

The crux of Ellis' (1977) theory was his contention that individuals often make irrational interpretations of situations and events, which are based on one of the eleven irrational beliefs that are common in our society. These irrational ideas, (B), cause the anxiety and related negative behaviors.

Lets review the first example:

A—going to a party attended by many strangers.

C—feeling tense and anxious, drinking too much too quickly.

Put yourself in this situation and try to decide what you might be saying to yourself about going to the party that would create anxiety. Several possibilities exist. You may be telling yourself that you have to appear perfectly competent and "cool" when you meet new people, that you have to make a good impression. Or, you may be saying to yourself that everyone at the party must like you and therefore you must be a sparkling conversationalist.

All of these statements, B, are irrational and put pressure on you. Thus, not the party itself, but the irrational beliefs and expectations that you are putting on yourself cause the anxiety.

In the second example:

A—not being productive on the job.

C—a vague sense of anxiety, dissatisfaction, and increased work absences.

Ask yourself what you might be saying to yourself about (A), being less productive at work. As in the previous example a number of possibilities exist. Perhaps you are telling yourself that you have to be extremely productive all of the time in order to be an adequate worker, or maybe you are telling yourself that this period of low productivity is an absolute disaster from which you can never recover. You might even be telling yourself that this period of low productivity is just another failure that is part of a repeating pattern of failures that has repeated itself since childhood.

The net result of all of these irrational statements is not only anxiety. Your chances of facing the problem squarely and doing something about it are decreased greatly by anxiety and irrational thinking.

The ABC system involves use of the following definitions:

A—The event or situation

B—Statement/interpretation/belief that gives positive or negative meaning to the event or situation

C—Anxiety and resulting negative behaviors

The best way to learn to identify your own irrational beliefs is to practice analyzing your anxiety feelings by using the ABC method. Remember to refer to the previous list of eleven irrational ideas. Missing the underlying irrational idea by focusing on a superficial idea that really is not at the heart of the anxiety is possible. For example, if the event, A, is taking a difficult exam, and the consequence, C, is fear and anxiety, the irrational belief is not that you might flunk the test. This belief may or may not be irrational; however, your beliefs about how well you must perform and how awful it would be if you fail are the irrational ideas responsible for your anxiety. The typical response that you might get from a friend in this kind of situation could be, "Oh, don't worry, you'll do all right." This response is not helpful because it really does not challenge the underlying irrational belief—that it would be a tragedy if you failed.

Challenging Irrational Beliefs

To challenge irrational beliefs, you need to know something about how you typically are persuaded to change an idea or opinion. Do you tend to respond to logic and fact? If so, you should try to argue with yourself from a factual, logical perspective. Or perhaps you are a more emotional kind of person and you respond more to value/affect oriented arguments. Do you tend to like gentle persuasion, or do you listen to forceful, emphatic statements? These distinctions may seem silly when you actually are referring to a process where you argue with yourself;

but, as you will understand when you try it, you need every tool you can find to overcome strongly ingrained irrational ideas.

In addition to knowing something about your own style of persuasion, reviewing general arguments against each of the eleven irrational statements is helpful also. Following are examples of several arguments against two of the irrational statements:

1. It is a dire necessity for an adult human being to be loved or approved by virtually everyone in his community. (Ellis, 1962, p. 61)

a. You can't expect everyone to like everyone else.

b. To have personal conflicts with some people is only human.

c. To be loved and approved is nice, but you don't need approval from everyone.

d. Sometimes you have to be selfish and do things that others don't like.

e. You can't spend your life always pleasing others.

2. One should be thoroughly competent, adequate, and achieving in all possible respects if one is to consider oneself worthwhile. (Ellis, 1962, p. 63)

a. Nobody can do everything well.

b. To make mistakes is human.

c. You can be a capable human being and not be good at a particular activity.

d. Honest effort is good, but you shouldn't feel guilty if you sometimes aren't perfectly competent.

e. People like you and find you worthwhile for a variety of reasons other than your level of achievement and competence.

In the activities section of this chapter you will have a chance to develop a list of your own arguments against the different irrational ideas. Developing strategies to challenge your listed ideas will be a phase of the activities.

Consider the value of asking a person with whom you share your inner feelings and thoughts to respond to your irrational statements. An insightful friend can help you identify an irrational thought or assumption in a way that may help you challenge a heretofore unchallengeable idea. Remember to find your own challenging process; be creative. Perhaps recording your irrational thoughts will help. Sometimes seeing something in black and white can be useful. Try to think about your irrational beliefs when you are in a setting that is relaxing to you. Often a vacation or break from your regular routine will help you get better insight into your own belief system.

Modifying Irrational Beliefs

You do not have to change your beliefs radically to be more rational. Usually, it is just a question of moving from absolutes. Take, for example, irrational belief number one:

It is a dire necessity for an adult human being to be loved or approved by virtually every other significant person in his/her community.

Let us assume you have successfully challenged this statement—You know that everyone does not have to like you and that in fact you can live quite a comfortable life with some people even disliking you. So, to modify this statement you might change it to read—human beings are social creatures and they like to be loved and approved, but they also are strong enough to stand by themselves when necessary. By changing the irrational form of this statement to a rational one you decrease the anxiety associated with the need to be liked by everyone. If you go to a party attended by many strangers, you can admit to yourself that some people will not like you—they may even find you boring. But that is okay because you do not need everyone to like you.

Practicing Rational Beliefs

Practice is crucial if you want to learn how to use this method as an anxiety management technique. Understanding alone is not enough. You have to analyze regularly and, challenge your irrational beliefs. If you consistently work on challenging the beliefs that underlie your anxiety, you eventually will develop what Ellis (1962) called a rational philosophy of life. You will find yourself feeling anxious less often because your thinking has become more rational and you have generally modified your irrational belief system.

SUMMARY

1. According to Albert Ellis, many anxieties are caused not by events, but by the way one views events.

2. The cognitive approach to anxiety management can be used to complement the physical relaxation and the health-oriented methods previously studied.

3. Many common irrational beliefs are a result of our competitive, yet highly socialized, society.

4. Your own irrational beliefs are a result of how you learned to view the world as a child and as a young adult.

5. An understanding of your particular irrational beliefs and how you learned them can help you modify them.

6. An effective method for analyzing irrational beliefs is to use the ABC model, with A—situation or event, B—underlying beliefs, and C—anxiety and negative behaviors.

7. The difficult part is in identifying irrational beliefs. A natural tendency is to believe that an event, (A), causes anxiety, (C), so that (B), the irrational belief is sometimes hard to determine.

8. Anxiety and negative behavior caused by irrational thinking often prevent you from working toward an effective solution to a problem.

9. Although identifying your irrational beliefs is an important step, you still have to find a way to challenge and change these beliefs.

10. Following these four steps, (a) identify, (b) challenge, (c) modify, and (d) practice, will enable you to change irrational beliefs.

11. To challenge effectively an irrational belief you have to be able to understand and accept the fact that the particular belief is irrational.

12. Various forms of persuasion can be used to help you understand this irrationality. Internal self dialogue and discussions with others are helpful.

13. Irrational beliefs are often irrational because of their absolute quality, so modifying irrational beliefs to make them rational usually means developing an absolute statement.

14. If you consistently challenge irrational beliefs, you will eventually develop a more rational, less anxiety producing general belief system.

SELF-ASSESSMENT
DISCUSSION QUESTIONS

1. Is thinking significant in your own anxiety process?

2. What do you think about Ellis' contention that society tends to teach people irrational beliefs?

3. Do you agree with Ellis about the irrationality of his eleven statements?

4. Which of the irrational statements are you most likely to use? How would you restate these statements in your own words?

5. Which of the irrational statements are more likely to be used by men? Women?

6. Can you identify how you learned the irrational statements that you are most prone to use?

7. Can the situation or event, (A), be an imagined event or situation?

8. Is the anxiety, labeled (C), in the ABC equation always accompanied by negative behaviors?

9. Can the elimination of irrational thinking help you work toward the solution of a problem situation?

10. What is meant by underlying irrational beliefs?

11. Identify several ways to challenge irrational beliefs. Which ways work best for you?

12. Why is it desirable to challenge irrational beliefs consistently?

13. Is it possible to be ambitious and achievement oriented without being irrational?

14. Is it possible to believe that the affection and love from others are important and still be rational?

15. How do values relate to irrational thinking?

ACTIVITIES

Activity 7.1 UNDERSTANDING IRRATIONAL BELIEFS

Purpose: Explore how individual irrational beliefs develop.

Instructions: Choose three of Ellis's eleven irrational statements that you are most likely to use. Write each on the top of a sheet of paper. Then do the following:

1. Restate the irrational belief in at least two different ways.

2. List some of the ways you think you have learned this belief; if you can, include a statement about whether this belief is held by other family members.

3. Write several statements challenging each irrational belief.

4. Restate each irrational belief as a rational belief.

Activity 7.2 PRACTICING THE ABC METHOD

Purpose: Learn to apply the ABC method.

Instructions: During a period of several days manage your anxiety by analyzing and modifying your irrational beliefs. Keep a log and record the following items according to the ABC method:

1. Situation or event, (A) (time, place, other people, etc.);

2. Anxiety, (C), (type of anxiety felt and related negative behaviors);

3. Irrational thinking, (B) (sentences that you are saying to yourself that cause anxiety);

4. Statements challenging your irrational thinking;

5. Restatement of irrational thoughts, (C), into rational statements.

If you are working on anxiety management with a group or with another person, discuss situations recorded in your log with someone.

Activity 7.3 UNDERLYING IRRATIONAL BELIEFS

Purpose: Practice identifying and challenging irrational beliefs.

Instructions: Analyze the following anxiety situations and list irrational statements that might be involved. After you have listed as many irrational statements as possible, develop strategies for challenging the irrational statements that you have listed.

1. Situation A, telling a close friend that he/she cannot borrow $50 from you.

Consequence C, feel anxious and avoid seeing this friend.

2. Situation A, having sex with someone you have been dating whom you like very much.

Consequence C, nervous/anxious, unable to enjoy the sexual contact.

3. Situation A, learning that your spouse is having an affair.

Consequence C, panic, hysteria, being immobilized.

4. Situation A, your boss telling you that although you are next in line, someone else is going to get the promotion that you have expected.

Consequence C, tension, anger, impulse to quit.

5. Situation A, telephoning someone you have met briefly to ask if he/she would like to have dinner with you.

Consequence C, anxiety, fear, shakey voice when talking.

BIBLIOGRAPHY

Ellis, A. *Reason and emotion in psychotherapy.* New York: Lyle Stuart, 1962. Paperback edition, New York: Citadel, 1977.

Ellis, A., & Harper, R. A. *A new guide to rational living.* Englewood Cliffs, New Jersey: Prentice-Hall, and Hollywood: Wilshire Books, 1975.

Positive self-statements can help you cope with performance anxiety.

Chapter 8

STRESS INOCULATION

Remember when you were a child and you had your first vaccination? You asked your mother why that scratch on your arm protected you from smallpox and she told you that it gave you a very mild case of smallpox. Of course, this information was confusing, because how could getting smallpox help your not getting smallpox? You learned, perhaps sometime later, that the minor case of smallpox from the vaccine helped your body develop a defense against the disease by creating antibodies that would remain in your body to fight the disease in the future.

Meichenbaum (1977) developed a method of combating stress that is based upon the same principle. In his method you learn anxiety coping skills by rehearsing stressful situations and your response to them. Thus, you become inoculated against stress so that when you are in a real situation you already have developed effective ways to manage the anxiety.

LEARNING STRESS INOCULATION

Stress inoculation involves the development of positive thoughts, self-statements, and use of cue-controlled muscle relaxation. The cognitive component is similar to Ellis' (1977) approach (Chapter 7), except that the focus is on self-statements related to specific stress situations rather than on underlying beliefs and assumptions. For example, if you are anxious about giving a speech, Ellis (1977) would have you analyze your irrational beliefs about how you think you should perform the speech. He also would have you analyze how failing or not living up to your expectations affects you. In stress inoculation you would be trying to modify negative self-statements directly by substituting positive coping self-statements. If you are anxious about a speech, for example, you would develop a set of positive coping statements that you could use when you begin to feel worried and anxious. The stress inoculation method also includes active deep muscle relaxation so that you combat your anxiety on both a physical and mental level.

Coping Versus Mastery

In stress inoculation you are encouraged to use and to accept a coping rather than a mastery model. That is, you learn that experiencing stress is normal and that often just coping with a tough situation means you have managed your anxiety effectively. By learning to cope with situations, you experience and manage anxiety. If you expect to master every anxiety situation so that you are in total control and feel no anxiety, you probably are doomed to failure. In essence you set for yourself an impossible task. Learning to manage and to cope with anxiety is more realistic and ultimately more anxiety reducing than striving to eliminate anxiety responses.

Positive Self-Statements

Meichenbaum (1977) divided anxiety reactions into four stages:

1. preparing for a stressor,
2. confronting and handling a stressor,
3. coping with the feeling of being overwhelmed, and
4. reinforcing self-statements (1977, p. 155).

In order to use stress inoculation you develop and memorize a set of self-statements to be used for each stage. According to Meichenbaum the use of these self-statements can help the user to

1. assess the reality of the situation;
2. control negative thoughts and images;
3. acknowledge, use, and relabel the arousal the user is experiencing;
4. "psych" oneself to confront the phobic situation;
5. cope with the intense fear that might be experienced; and

6. reflect on one's performance and reinforce self for having coped. (1977, p. 155)

114

Stage 1–Preparing for a Stressor. This stage focuses on self-statements made any time prior to confronting stressful situations. This period varies according to how much time a person spends preparing for a stressor, some situations may involve several days or weeks and others may involve just a few hours. Meichenbaum listed several possible coping self-statements for this stage.

1. What is it you have to do?

2. Can you develop a plan to deal with it?

3. Just think about what you can do about it, that is better than getting anxious.

4. No negative self-statements; just think rationally.

5. Do not worry; worry will not help anything.

6. Maybe what you think is anxiety is eagerness to confront the situation. (1977, p. 155)

These statements are aimed at helping you do two things: first, to focus on specific preparation for the task; and second, to combat negative thinking and self-statements. By emphasizing planning and preparation you redirect the energy it takes to worry and fret into specific action that helps you become better prepared for a stressful situation. This action focus also stops you from becoming immobilized by the fear that can be produced by negative statements such as, "It is going to be awful," or "I cannot do it." All specific statements, like more general ones, focus on preparation and block worry and negative statements.

Notice that Meichenbaum's (1977) sample positive coping self-statements can be applied to any anxiety situation. You can also tailor self-statements to specific situations that elicit anxiety for you. Some examples of specific coping statements for Stage 1, preparing for a stressor, are presented for three different situations.

Situation A: Anxiety about telephoning someone for a date.

1. What am I going to say first?

2. Instead of putting it off, I am just going to do it.

115

3. It will be okay once I start talking.

4. I can take it if he/she says "no."

5. Stop worrying about him/her saying "no." It wouldn't be so awful.

Situation B: Anxiety about starting a new job.

1. What can I do to get acclimated as quickly as possible?

2. I don't have to know everything right away.

3. Stop worrying, things will go just fine.

4. Once I arrive, I'll be okay.

Situation C: Fear of driving in heavy rush-hour traffic.

1. I will be okay if I just do not get rattled.

2. I know exactly where I'm going.

3. I'll give myself plenty of time.

4. I don't have to hurry.

5. I've planned my route.

Stage 2—Confronting and handling a stressor. This stage of an anxiety reaction occurs when you actually confront the stress situation. Miechenbaum suggested the following general coping self-statements.

1. Just "psych" yourself up; you can meet this challenge.

2. You can convince yourself to do it. You can reason your fear away.

3. One step at a time; you can handle the situation.

4. Do not think about fear; just think about what you have to do. Stay relevant.

5. This anxiety is what the doctor said you would feel. It is a reminder to use your coping exercises.

6. This tenseness can be an ally: a cue to cope.

7. Relax; you are in control. Take a slow deep breath. Ah, good. (1977, p.155)

In Stage 2 the self-statements are designed to help you first to relax (cue the relaxation response); second, to reassure yourself that you *can* handle the situation; and third, to rein?terpret the anxiety as something that you can use. The coping self-statement related to relaxing is very important because it triggers a physical relaxation response.

Following are specific coping self-statements for Stage 2, confronting a stressor, for the previous situations A, B, and C.

Situation A: Anxiety about telephoning someone for a date.

1. Just concentrate on your first couple of sentences.

2. Go ahead, dial the number.

3. Focus on what you are going to say, not the fear.

4. Some anxiety is okay, it won't hurt anything.

Situation B: Anxiety about starting a new job.

1. It is okay to be nervous at first.

2. Go on in, concentrate on being friendly to people.

3. Remember they don't expect you to know much at first.

4. Take a deep breath and go on in.

5. Be assertive, introduce yourself to people.

Situation C: Fear of driving in heavy, rush-hour traffic.

1. Just concentrate on your driving.

2. Don't hurry.

3. Don't let crazy drivers rattle you.

4. You're in control.

5. Some anxiety is okay, it will not cause you to lose control.

Some of these specific coping self-statements refer to the particular situation (Just concentrate on your driving). while others relate more to your own particular anxiety response (Do not hurry). When you are constructing positive coping statements, think about your own anxiety reactions. If you have a tendency to hurry and feel pressed for time when you are trying to cope, the command "Don't hurry" will be helpful. If you often feel as if you are going to lose control and are frightened by that prospect, then a statement such as "You are in control" will be useful. Also, if specific statements such as, "Take a deep breath . . . ," help trigger your relaxation response use them to help with physical relaxation.

Stage 3—Coping With the Feeling Of Being Overwhelmed. This stage does not necessarily occur, that is you do not always reach a point where you feel as if you are being overwhelmed. However, by developing positive coping statements to use if you do begin to feel overwhelmed you will be preparing for all possibilities. This preparation in itself is useful because it helps you realize that you are prepared to deal with the worst situation—feeling out of control and overwhelmed. Meichenbaum suggested the following general positive coping self-state?ments for this stage:

1. When fear comes, just pause.

2. Keep the focus on the present; what is it you have to do.

3. Label your fear from 0 to 10 and watch fear change.

4. Do not try to eliminate fear totally; just keep it manageable.

5. You should expect your fear to rise. (1977, p. 155)

As with the two earlier stages—preparing for a stressor and confronting a stressor—you can develop coping statements for stage 3 that are specific to a particular anxiety situation. Examples of some of these specific statements for the three same previous sample situations follow:

118

Situation A: Anxiety about telephoning someone for a date.

1. Just pause for a minute, you will be able to talk.

2. That first sentence is the hardest, then conversation will get easier.

3. Being scared is okay, you can still function.

4. If you have to do so, you can excuse yourself for a minute to take a deep breath.

Situation B: Anxiety about starting a new job.

1. You may be frightened at first, but you can still continue.

2. The strong fear will pass, concentrate on doing or learning something.

Situation C: Fear of driving in heavy, rush-hour traffic.

1. You won't lose control, just focus on your driving.

2. Your anxiety is at its peak; it will decrease now.

3. Take a breath, pause, and then focus on your driving.

In addition to developing coping statements related to being overcome by fear, make specific plans concerning how you might handle the situation. These plans help you in two ways. First, they prevent anxiety because you learn that you have some control even if the worst happens and you become overwhelmed. Second, these plans give you an escape mechanism if you need it. For example, if you get so overwhelmed when telephoning for a date that you cannot talk, you can excuse yourself for a few minutes, or even hang up, regain some composure, then recall, and finish the conversation. Or, if you absolutely cannot function because of fears about a new job, you can take a coffee break, go to the bathroom, or even talk to one of your new fellow employees about your fear.

Some risk is involved in planning ways to escape being overwhelmed, particularly if you develop a pattern of avoiding situations. If you never drive in rush-hour traffic, you avoid the anxiety. You also limit your mobility and in a sense allow anxiety to control part of your life. Try to spend your energies on learning how to cope rather than how to escape.

Stage 4—Reinforcing Self-statements. Most individuals get through situations that cause great anxiety, but how many give themselves a pat on the back for having coped? Think about the difference between the following two self-statements a person might make after overcoming a great fear of telephoning someone for a date:

a. Whew, . . . I am glad that is over. I did pretty well. She is going to go out with me.

b. Oh! . . . I was so nervous. She said "yes," but I know I sounded like an idiot.

Statement "a" is positive and reinforcing, while statement "b" is negative and probably will produce additional anxiety. Statement "a" will make calling a little easier the next time and probably will prevent building up too much anxiety about the date itself. Statement "b" on the other hand, accentuates the negative. Underlying statement "b" is the assumption that coping with the situation is not enough, the situation has to be mastered instead. The dangers of this need for perfection should be obvious at this point.

Meichenbaum suggested several general positive *self-reinforcing* statements for this final stage:

1. It worked; you did it.
2. Wait until you tell your therapist (or group) about this.
3. It was not as bad as you expected.
4. You made more out of your fear than it was worth.
5. Your damn ideas, that is the problem. When you control them, you control your fear.
6. It is getting better each time you use the procedures.
7. You can be pleased with the progress you are making.
8. You did it! (1977, p. 155)

The most important function of these statements is to *reinforce* your efforts to manage anxiety. You may not realize that your own self-statements can be powerful reinforcers. As in the other stages, these positive statements also help you decrease and eventually eliminate negative, non-reinforcing self-statements.

In this final stage the *specific* statements probably are not as important as in the other three stages. One can use general reinforcing self-statements for any situation, or use a kind of fill-in-the-blank:

1. I did it! I (got a date).

2. Congratulations, you (drove in rush-hour traffic).

REHEARSING POSITIVE COPING STATEMENTS AND RELAXATION

After you have developed and memorized a set of positive self-statements including both general and specific statements, you are ready to rehearse using these statements. As you rehearse, remember also to use the active deep muscle relaxation response that you learned in Chapter 5 as you begin to confront the stressor. In order to learn to rehearse the self-statements and the muscle relaxation response, you should simulate the real anxiety situation as much as possible. You may be able to imagine the four stages with specific anxiety situations in mind: (1) preparing for a stressor; (2) confronting and handling a stressor; (3) coping with the feeling of being overwhelmed; and (4) reinforcing self-statements. If you are trying to manage your anxiety reaction when you meet new people, set up an imaginary scenario in which you are going to meet a new person. As you visualize the scene in your mind, practice the coping statements and relaxation. The following examples will help to illustrate how to do this.

Situation D: Starting a conversation with a stranger.

Imaginary Scene	Practice Coping
1. You are approaching someone you want to get to know.	1. Coping statements for preparing for a stressor stage.
2. You sit next to the person.	2. Coping statements for confronting and handling a stressor stage and muscle relaxation.
3. You begin a conversation, but anxiety begins to overwhelm you.	3. Coping statements for coping with the feeling of being overwhelmed.
4. Your conversation is over and you are walking away.	4. Reinforcing self-statements.

121

Situation E: Taking a difficult exam.

Imaginary Scene

1. Two days before the exam you start to worry about the test.

2. You are on your way to the exam. You begin the exam.

3. You come to a series of questions that you can't answer.

4. You walk out of the testing room.

Practice Coping

1. Coping statements for preparing for a stressor.

2. Coping statements for confronting and handling a stressor stage and muscle relaxation.

3. Coping statements for the feeling of being overwhelmed.

4. Reinforcing self? statements.

After you have practiced with imaginary scenes, try out the technique in a real setting. If you would be likely to talk with a stranger at a coffee shop, go to a coffee shop and practice your statements. After you have practiced relaxation and coping statements in various settings, you can begin to use them in actual anxiety situations. Aim for a kind of automatic coping mechanism that you can use in any difficult anxiety situation.

SUMMARY

1. Stress inoculation is a way of inoculating persons by having them develop and practice ways of coping with stress.

2. Stress inoculation involves the use of positive self-statements and a cue-controlled muscle relaxation response.

3. A coping versus mastery approach to anxiety situations is emphasized in this approach.

4. Meichenbaum (1977) suggested dividing anxiety reactions into four stages: (a) preparing for a stressor, (b) confronting and handling a stressor, (c) coping with the feeling of being overwhelmed, and (d) reinforcing self-statements.

5. By developing and learning coping self-statements for each stage, you can help yourself manage anxiety by: (a) assessing the reality of the situation, (b) controlling negative thoughts and images, (c) using anxiety positively, (d) "psych" yourself to confront situations, (e) cope with intense fear, and (f) reinforce yourself for having coped.

6. In the preparing for a stressor stage, positive self-statements help to focus on specific preparation for the task and also to combat negative thinking and self-statements.

7. The two kinds of coping self-statements are specific statements and general statements. Specific statements refer to specific anxiety situations while general statements can be used to cope with any situation.

8. Learning specific statements is helpful if you have a special situation that frequently causes anxiety.

9. A repetoire of general self-statements will help you manage predictable and unpredictable anxiety situations.

10. In the confronting a stressor stage positive self-statements help you: (a) relax physically, (b) reassure yourself that you *can* handle the situation, and (c) reinterpret the anxiety as something that you can use.

11. The relaxation statements help trigger your physical relaxation response.

12. Although you may not need this stage in every situation, the coping with the feeling of being overwhelmed stage helps you prepare for your worst fear, being overwhelmed and out of control. Basically, these statements help you focus on something else and decrease your fear to a manageable level.

13. Making contingency plans for what you would do if you *were* overwhelmed also is helpful, e.g., how you would escape, what you would say, or what you would do.

14. After you have developed positive coping statements for (a) preparing for a stressor, (b) confronting and handling a stressor, (c) possibly being overwhelmed by a stressor, you need to develop a set of statements to (d) reinforce yourself for having coped with the situation.

15. After memorizing positive self-statements, rehearse using them in a variety of anxiety situations.

16. As a first step try using coping statements and relaxation to cope with anxiety situations that you imagine.

17. The next rehearsal step is to try the statements and relaxation in the physical setting while imagining the situation.

18. After you have practiced and rehearsed sufficiently, you are ready to use stress inoculation in a real anxiety situation.

SELF-ASSESSMENT
DISCUSSION QUESTIONS

1. How often do you use negative self-statements in anxiety situations? What are some of your typical statements?

2. What is the difference between coping and mastery in relation to anxiety situations?

3. Why do positive coping self-statements help you manage anxiety?

4. Do you spend much time preparing for specific stress situations? Is the preparation positive or negative?

5. Does the preparation help you to focus on what has to be done when you are feeling very anxious about something?

6. What is the difference between specific and general positive self-statements?

7. What do you do to take your mind off worrying when you find yourself worrying about an upcoming situation?

8. Do you ever try to relax physically just when you are confronting a stressor? How?

9. Do you have any typical negative or positive self-statements that you use when confronting a stressor?

10. What do positive self-statements in the confronting and handling a stressor stage accomplish?

11. Can you describe what the feeling of being overwhelmed is like for you? Have you ever been overwhelmed by anxiety?

12. What is the value of planning what you would do if you were overwhelmed?

13. How difficult is formulating positive self-reinforcing statements for you? How do you feel when you pat yourself on the back for coping effectively?

14. Why are reinforcing self-statements so important?

15. Can you imagine stress situations vividly enough to feel some anxiety?

16. What rehearsal methods would work best for you?

ACTIVITIES

Activity 8.1 ANALYZING SELF-STATEMENTS

Purpose: To identify positive and negative self-statements and to learn the four stages of an anxiety reaction.

Instructions: Keep a log of the self-statements that you use currently to cope with anxiety situations, include positive and negative . After four or five days analyze your log and try to put your statements into these four stages: (a) preparing for a stressor, (b) confronting and handling a stressor, (c) coping with the feeling of being overwhelmed, and (d) reinforcing self-statements. Cross out negative statements and add positive cues until you have at least four positive statements for each stage.

Activity 8.2 USING STRESS INOCULATION

Purpose: To learn how to use stress inoculation as an anxiety management method.

Instructions: Write and memorize four positive self-statements for each of the four stages. Practice using the stages along with deep muscle relaxation whenever you encounter an anxiety producing situation. Keep a log of your reactions to each situation. Discuss your reactions with a friend or a small group.

Activity 8.3 COPING WITH PERFORMANCE ANXIETY

Purpose: To practice the stress inoculation method.

Instructions: After all members in the group have memorized and practiced positive self-statements and muscle relaxation, extend the use of the method by doing the following:

1. Have each group member indicate which of the following situations would elicit the most anxiety:

a. sing a song in front of the group,

b. do a dance in front of the group, or

c. make an extemporaneous speech.

2. Have each person perform his/her song, dance, speech, and practice stress inoculation responses to help cope with performance anxiety.

3. Discuss reactions to using stress inoculation in their anxiety producing situation.

BIBLIOGRAPHY

Ellis, A. *Reason and emotion in psychotherapy.* New York: Lyle Stuart, 1962. Paperback edition, New York: Citadel, 1977.

Meichenbaum, D. *Cognitive-behavior modification: An integrative approach.* New York: Plenum Press, 1977.

Meichenbaum, D. A self-instructional approach to stress management: A proposal for stress inoculation training. In C. Spielberger and I. Sarason (Eds.). *Stress and anxiety in modern life.* New York: Winston and Sons, 1979.

PART IV

LIFE STYLE
ISSUES AND ANXIETY

PART IV

LIFE STYLE
ISSUES AND ANXIETY

Up to this point the emphasis has been on teaching you how to manage anxiety by analyzing and modifying the physical and mental roles of your anxiety process. In this section you will examine how anxiety influences a number of life choices and events. The purpose is primarily to help you understand better how different aspects of your life style are related to anxiety and to increase your ability to make life choices that allow you to decrease excessive anxiety.

In Chapter 9 anxiety related to interpersonal relationships is explored. The importance of good social interaction skills, a capacity for intimacy, and assertiveness is described and suggestions for growth in these areas are presented.

In Chapter 10 the relationship between values and anxiety is discussed. Particular attention is given to value clarification, changing and conflicting values, conflicts between values and behavior, and lack of commitment.

In Chapter 11 connection among personality, attitudes toward time, and anxiety is described. You will have an opportunity to assess your own personal attitudes toward time and to learn about Type A behavior.

In Chapter 12, the last chapter of the unit, life transitions and anxiety will be examined. A brief discussion of anxiety role in normal developmental growth and in unplanned life transitions will be presented with suggestions for managing interfering anxiety.

Chapter 9

ANXIETY AND INTERPERSONAL RELATIONSHIPS

People who need people may be the luckiest in the world, but they also may be the most anxious. Anxiety is a part of most human relationships. The need that we all have for others makes us vulnerable, and that vulnerability gives relationships the potential for being both rewarding and anxiety producing. Anxiety is a normal part of social interactions; yet, in the extreme anxiety can be dehabilitating and block a person from the richness of being with others.

Think about your own attitudes and feelings towards others. Are you frequently nervous about what others say or about what you say? Do you have people around who love you and to whom you can turn for support and comfort? Do you swallow your feelings and move away from conflict feeling as if you will explode? Do you go home at night and experience a kind of chronic loneliness?

Being truthful with yourself about these issues is not easy; however, if you can identify and accept fears and anxieties, you will be able to take the first step toward improvement. Remember that no one has perfect, anxiety-free relationships. In fact relationships without the creative force of conflict and anxiety would be boring and lifeless. Excessive anxiety however often interferes with effective relationships. If relationships seem to cause too much anxiety for you, or if anxiety prevents you from having good relationships, the following information will be very helpful.

131

Three different approaches to managing relationship related anxiety are presented in this chapter: (1) Increasing general social interaction skills, (2) Improving one's capacity for intimacy, and (3) Learning to be assertive.

GENERAL INTERACTION SKILLS

General social interaction skills make accomplishing day-to-day transactions with people possible. These skills enable an individual to exchange small talk with strangers, to listen and understand what people are saying, to communicate something of and about oneself to others, and to form and maintain facilitative relationships. Poor interaction skills make it much more difficult to manage normal relationships. Anxiety about interactions often is caused by uncertainty that comes from lack of skill and experience. People who are shy, for example, often do not feel comfortable in general social interactions because they are not confident of their general interaction skills. These skills can be divided into four areas:

1. ability to listen actively,
2. ability to make small talk—to begin and sustain conversations,
3. ability to relate effectively in group situations, and
4. ability to self-disclose.

Active Listening

The ability to listen actively is a key to general success in relationships. Frequently, individuals are so intent upon getting their own point across that they just do not pay attention to what someone else is saying. When someone does really listen, it is meaningful. To listen actively you focus your attention on the other person. If you try to understand what the other person is saying and feeling, you will be taking an important first step in active listening.

To achieve this kind of understanding you must perceive the situation from the other person's frame of reference, put yourself in the other person's shoes so to speak. This process is called empathy. To listen actively you must be able to empathize (understand from the other person's point of view) and to communicate that empathic understanding. Your nonverbal behavior is as important as what you say. Your facial expressions, head nods, eye contact, body position, and body movements all tell the other person how actively you are listening.

132

Researchers have determined that increasing one's ability to listen actively and to communicate empathy is possible. The simplest and most direct way to improve these skills is to practice and then to solicit feedback from others. This practicing may be somewhat difficult because you may not be accustomed to asking people for direct feedback. Social convention often prevents you from getting honest opinions from others, so choosing a person willing to give you both positive and negative feedback is essential.

Formal opportunities to improve general social interaction skills also are available. Opportunities for communications skill training or empathy training abound at local colleges, churches, and personal growth centers. Several active listening exercises also are provided at the end of this chapter.

Small Talk

One often hears people say, "I hate to make small talk, it is so meaningless." But it is not meaningless! Small talk is the ritual that people use to make contact with each other. Yes, it is superficial, but it is also an important stage in establishing relationships. The content or words exchanged are not as important as the general interaction that occurs. In a sense the words allow the interpersonal process to begin. Many people avoid interpersonal contacts, particularly with new people because they are anxious or negative about small talk.

If you increase your skill at making small talk and interacting comfortably on a relatively superficial level, you possibly will find your interpersonal anxiety decreased and the range of your relationships increased. Two strategies can be helpful. One strategy is to build your repertoire of small talk. Start by making a list of opening lines that might work in a variety of circumstances. The following openings are some examples:

Haven't I seen you at (give name of place)?

It is a gorgeous (dreadful, nice, etc.) day, isn't it?

Have you been here before?

Where do you jog/play tennis/go to school/etc? (Depending upon what the person is carrying or wearing—jogging outfit, tennis racket, books, etc.).

133

Hi, how are you doing today?

Do you work, go to school?

Do you live around here? Been in this area long?

How do you like San Francisco, Omaha, etc. so far? (If you know the person has arrived recently.)

What do you think of the situation in (supply the specific)?

That business in (name the place, thing, or activity) is really (awful, great, interesting) isn't it?

Creating an all inclusive list is impossible because the context of each situation is different. What you would say at a party is different from what you would say to someone you are sitting beside on the bus. Remember to keep in mind that what you say is really just a vehicle for making contact. People, of course, will not always reciprocate. If you are sitting next to someone on a plane, you ask a question or make a comment and get an abrupt answer followed by a hasty return to United Airlines magazine, that is probably a signal that the person does not want to interact. That happens sometimes and is perfectly okay. Although learning some "lines" can be helpful, your interest in others has to be genuine. You must have a real interest and willingness to learn about the other person.

As a second strategy for dealing with anxiety related to small talk, you can use some of the techniques that you learned previously. A deep breath and a positive self-statement may give you just enough confidence to move into a new interpersonal situation.

Relating in Group Situations

A group situation is one that causes particular difficulties for some individuals. Often anxiety about being in groups comes from fear of group expectations or of potential negative appraisal by other group members. A group can consist of from three to several hundred people. Usually however when a group causes anxiety it consists of just a few people.

An improvement in general social interaction skills will help decrease anxiety about groups. Also, experiences in minimal threatening groups such as clubs, organizations, and other structured groups can help build self-confidence and decrease anxiety.

Self-Disclosure

In all of these general interaction skill areas you have to be willing to share part of yourself. When you practice active listening, your communication of empathy requires you to risk telling the other person your perception of his/her feelings. At times you may even share your feelings or experiences in similar situations. When you are making small talk, you have to contribute something eventually about yourself. The level of your self-disclosure has a decided effect on where the conversation goes next. Self-disclosure also is essential in intimate relationships. In these relationships you have to be able to disclose feelings that may be difficult and risky to express.

INTIMACY

Intimate relationships are different in many respects from general social interactions. Relationship skills are less important than the personal capacity to love, to be loved, and to risk the possibility of rejection. Although intimate relationships frequently are thought of as sexual, being intimate with someone and choosing not to develop the sexual aspect of that relationship certainly is possible.

An intimate relationship usually develops with nurturing and is a process which involves a gradual lowering of defenses. A reciprocal relationship gradually forms so that a depth of communication and understanding makes each partner more and more secure. Few things in life are more rewarding or more personally validating. Naturally, with these kinds of rewards the risks are high.

An inability to form intimate relationships robs one of a powerful anxiety management tool—the care and support of a close friend or loved one. Conflict related to unsuccessful attempts to form intimate relationships also can create considerable excess anxiety. You can expect a certain amount of fear and anxiety when you are forming new intimate relationships. But if you find yourself experiencing a pattern of excess anxiety related to intimate relationships, you probably need to look at yourself and the way you react to intimacy.

Because intimacy problems are so complex, the possibility of adequately covering them in this general approach to anxiety management is limited. However, you can improve your awareness of intimacy related anxiety. The first question you should ask is whether you have any intimate relationships. Do you know people with whom you can really relax and be yourself? Do you have friends whom you trust explicitly and who also trust you in a similar way? Do you feel that some of your relationships are developing into intimate ones? Are you blocking this growth? Do fear and anxiety interfere?

No instant cures for intimacy fears and problems are available. Although some gurus and therapies seem to offer easy answers, the growth of intimacy is usually a fragile, hesitant process. Anxiety created by fear of rejection is a major part of the process and becomes a problem only if the fear interferes with the process itself.

ASSERTIVENESS

When you are overly cautious and elect not to express your wishes and feelings, you pay a price—anxiety. Even though you consciously may decide not to express yourself (and of course, many times this decision is appropriate), your body still responds. The emotional energy your body requires not to respond adds to already existing anxiety. Situations which stimulate you to express feelings and to be assertive happen frequently. Your college professor may refuse a legitimate request for an extension on a paper, a friend may continue to assume that you feel a certain way, or a car salesperson may treat you as if he/she thinks you are a dumb person. These examples go on and on.

All too frequently people choose not to express themselves and nonassertiveness becomes a pattern. A negative cycle develops and the individual starts to believe that he/she cannot be assertive or that he/she does not deserve to voice an opinion or feeling. The anxiety caused by nonassertiveness often is accompanied by strong anger. This anger is directed at others for not paying attention to nonassertive feelings about which other person(s) often are unaware and anger at him/herself for being wishy-washy and nonassertive.

This opposite is also true. Individuals can become so assertive that their total philosophy of life is selfish. This attitude violates the rights of others and general social interactions become disharmonious. The overassertive or aggressive person finds that because of his/her violation of others he/she is alienated.

136

Wolpe (1973) originally developed assertive training as a behavior modification technique designed to treat neurotic anxiety. He suggested that by teaching people to be assertive, a process called reciprocal inhibition would take place wherein the assertive behavior would in effect cancel out the anxiety response. Alberti and Emmons (1970) in their book, *Your Perfect Right,* popularized the concept so that today most people are exposed to some form of assertive training program at church, school, or some social organization. This popularization is generally a healthy development, except that some assertion proponents have gone overboard and tend to overemphasize the "me first" aspects of assertiveness leaving out the importance of respecting the other person's rights.

Alberti and Emmons (1970) suggested three possible ways of expressing feelings and desires: (1) nonassertive behavior, (2) aggressive behavior, and (3) assertive behavior. *Nonassertive behavior* essentially is being passive and not expressing your true feelings or wishes. If your spouse does not complete a household chore that he/she has agreed previously to do and you get very angry but do not say anything, you are being passive or nonassertive. If you scream and holler and throw oranges at your spouse, you are being *aggressive;* and if you express your anger and tell your spouse when and why you are angry, you are being *assertive.*

Anxiety most often comes with being nonassertive and not allowing yourself to express your feelings or assuming the responsibilities and consequences of assertiveness. Most assertive training programs begin with some discussion of attitudes. You have to believe in your right to be assertive and be willing to accept the corresponding responsibilities and consequences before you can change your behavior. Changing attitudes can be particularly difficult if you have developed a kind of passive "I will sacrifice" social role (a well reinforced feminine role). Discussion with others who are more assertive and have a positive philosophy toward others often helps foster attitudinal change. A cooperative, facilitative attitudes nutures self enhancement and self promotion. Assertiveness does not always mean struggle or against something, but can be a technique to create a nurturing environment.

After you come to believe that you are entitled to be assertive, all that remains is to learn how to be assertive. This involves learning appropriate kinds of responses (ways to express yourself), practicing them, first in controlled settings (role plays or with friends), and then moving out slowly into the real world.

The following steps will help you develop your own assertive behaviors:

1. Learn the difference between assertive, passive, and aggressive responses.

An understanding of how each kind of response (assertive, passive, aggressive) affects the person giving the response and the person or persons to whom the response is directed will help you realize why an assertive response is usually most desirable.

Generally, assertive responses allow you to express your own feelings and rights without violating the rights of another person. This expression helps counteract the anxiety that comes from holding in thoughts and feelings and permits the other person to know your honest reactions. Sometimes other persons may not seem to want to know your real reaction; however, over an extended time assertive behavior usually leads to more successful relationships.

Passive behavior, not expressing your feelings or thoughts, is harmful to everyone concerned. If you are passive, the chances are great that you experience anxiety as a result of choosing not to express yourself. Too much of this anxiety can be harmful in many ways. If you are passive continually in certain situations or toward certain people, you probably will build much resentment related to that person or that situation. This resentment can sour relationships or propel you into impulsive behavior that you may later regret.

A pattern of passive behavior also can lead to aggressive responses which carry the power of many earlier unexpressed feelings and thoughts. Generally aggressive behavior does not consider the other person's rights and it usually causes people toward whom it is directed to become defensive and noncooperative.

Studying these following three examples will help you learn to identify aggressive, passive, and assertive responses.

Example 1. *A man is angry with his wife because she scheduled a weekend social engagement with friends without telling him beforehand.*

Passive response—decides not to say anything because it will only lead to an argument.

138

Assertive response—tells his wife that he is hurt and angry because she made plans without discussing them with him.

Aggressive response—screams, calls his wife an inconsiderate shrew, storms out of the house, and gets loaded.

Example 2. *A daughter is talking with her mother on the phone. Her mother wants her to visit next weekend. The daughter has other plans and really does not want to visit then. She tries to say no, but her mother tells the daughter that she won't have too many more years to visit her dear old mother, and she better come as often as she can.*

Passive response—gives in and says she will cancel her other plans.

Assertive response—tells her mother she cannot come, that she already has made other plans.

Aggressive response—screams at her mother, telling her to stop trying to give her a guilt trip and hangs up the phone.

Example 3. *A teenage boy feels very affectionate towards his father who has just finished having a very helpful talk with him.*

Passive response—decides not to say or do anything because it might be embarrassing.

Assertive response—hugs his dad and tells him how much he loves him.

Aggressive response—runs to his father and cries hysterically that he (son) does not know how he (son) could manage without him (father).

2. Assess your own assertive, aggressive, and passive behavior.

Each individual, of course, chooses different response patterns at different times. The key to assessing your own behavior is to identify patterns. Are you usually passive with certain people or types of people? Do certain situations seem to make you overly passive? Are you usually aggressive? Probably the easiest way to get an accurate view of your behavior is to keep some kind of chart or diary of your daily interactions. After you have recorded several days action, you will be able to discern patterns. Remember to record how you are feeling when you respond or don't respond and also try to remember accurately how you respond. You may need to seek the help of a friend to check your understanding of these three kinds of responses.

3. Develop new assertive responses for specific situations.

After you have identified some of the patterns in your response behavior, you will be able to decide which kinds of situations and people that you need to develop responses. For example, if you find that you are usually passive around authority figures (like your boss, your professors, older men or women, etc.), you probably need to concentrate on developing assertive behavior with those kinds of people. Select at least three situations common to your experience with which to start. Write the situation and some of your typical responses. Then write several assertive responses that you would like to be able to use.

4. Think through and/or discuss the risks of being assertive in situations.

This step is very important because there are indeed risks to being assertive. Usually, assertive behavior is most effective, but at times it may have very negative consequences. For example, if you feel that your boss is totally ignorant and unqualified for his/her job. you may not want to take the risk of being assertive with those particular feelings. Or if you have been dissatisfied with your marriage for several years, asserting this dissatisfaction will certainly lead to some major confrontations and discussions with your spouse.

Thinking through these risks is tough because it is difficult to differentiate real risks from fears that you have been using as rationalizations for passive or aggressive behavior.

5. Rehearse your assertive behavior.

Try to visualize yourself in a particular situation making an assertive response. Do this while you are calm and relaxed so that you can begin to learn the response without experiencing undue anxiety. After you have rehearsed internally, set up a situation where you can role play the assertive response and get feedback about how you responded. Remember that the how is as important as what you say. Ask an observer to pay particular attention to what goes on nonverbally during your rehearsal.

6. Try out assertive responses in a real situation.

The ultimate goal of developing assertive behavior is using it in real life situations. If you are attempting to change a major behavior pattern, you may find that people are surprised and taken aback by your new assertive behavior. You may want to tell people who are close to you that you are making an effort to be more assertive and help them understand what this may mean in terms of your relationship with them. Giving them a kind of warning may help them adjust to your new behavior.

Try to remember also that you may initially need to provide support and reinforcement for yourself. Eventually however you will find that most people respond well to assertiveness. You will certainly feel less anxious at the moments when you are assertive, and also by not building up anxiety and anger through passive and/or aggressive behavior you will find that your overall level of anxiety decreases.

7. Maintain your assertive behavior by constant reevaluation and reinforcement.

It's easy to fall into bad habits. Even if your general pattern of responses is assertive, you may slip into nonassertive responses in certain situations or periods. After you become aware of the concept of assertiveness and of your own anxiety reactions it should be fairly easy for you to recognize when you are being passive or aggressive. It is particularly easy to be nonassertive about positive, affectionate responses. The anxiety that you feel is probably not as strong, but there is still an uneasy sense that you missed the time to express how you were feeling.

Remember that being assertive does not involve imposing your will on someone else. It does involve expressing your feelings, paying attention to your own rights, and being responsible for the consequences. These may at times come in conflict with other people's rights and feelings. Although this conflict can create a certain amount of anxiety, the chances are good that the conflict can be resolved without either party walking away with that tense, anxious feeling resulting from not expressing a strong feeling or opinion.

SUMMARY

1. Relationships with others are often anxiety producing because we all need other people and we care about how others react to us.

2. A critical self-examination can help you determine whether or not anxiety interferes with your own interpersonal relationships.

3. Although interpersonal behavior patterns frequently seem fixed, improving patterns and thereby decreasing interpersonal anxiety is possible.

4. Three different approaches to managing relationship-related anxiety are useful: (a) general social interaction skills, (b) intimacy, and (c) assertiveness.

5. People who do not have well developed general social interaction skills often experience considerable anxiety because they lack confidence in their abilities and because they avoid many interpersonal situations.

6. General social interaction skills can be divided into four skill areas: (a) ability to listen actively (express empathic understanding), (b) ability to make small talk—to begin and sustain conversation, (c) ability to relate effectively in group situations, and (d) self-disclosure.

7. Active listening, which involves listening empathically and being able to communicate that empathy is probably the most important general social interaction skill. The nonverbal aspects of active listening and expressing empathy also are critical. These behaviors include appropriate eye contact, body position, head nodding, facial expression, and gestures.

8. The best way to improve listening skills and emphatic understanding is to practice active listening and to receive honest feedback.

9. The content of small talk really is less important than the symbolic message, which is "I want to make contact with you."

10. If you are uncomfortable with small talk, memorizing and rehearsing a number of different "lines" can help decrease your anxiety and build your confidence.

11. Just memorizing lines is not enough. You will be much more successful interpersonally if you have a genuine interest in others.

12. Previously learned physical and cognitive anxiety management techniques are useful when dealing with interpersonal anxiety.

13. Anxiety about relating to members of groups can best be overcome by gaining experience in groups. Participation in structured groups where you can predict and control the extent of your involvement can be a helpful first step.

14. Intimate relationships always cause some anxiety because they require one to risk rejection. Anxiety becomes a problem when it consistently interferes with the development of intimate relationships.

15. Intimacy is less dependent upon skills and more dependent on a person's sense of identity, life style, and willingness to risk rejection.

16. Sex is often a part of intimate relationships, but not always. Intimacy is characterized by a deep sense of reciprocal love and trust.

17. The best way to work on intimacy problems is to talk with a sensitive friend or therapist. The first step is to become aware of your own willingness to form intimate relationships and of any blocks or difficulties that you encounter.

18. If you choose not to assert yourself, you pay a price in tension and anxiety. The energy that it takes to "swallow" your feelings increases your anxiety.

19. If you feel anxiety in a situation where you have not expressed yourself, the process of being assertive will cancel out the anxiety feelings.

20. Remember however that assertiveness is not overpowering someone else. It is expressing yourself while you respect the other person's rights.

21. The following steps will help you learn to be assertive:

a. Learn the difference between assertive, passive, and aggressive responses.

b. Assess your own assertive, passive, and aggressive behavior.

c. Develop new assertive responses for specific situations.

d. Think through and/or discuss the risks of being assertive in these situations.

e. Rehearse your assertive behavior.

f. Try out assertive responses in a real situation.

g. Maintain your assertive behavior by constant reevaluation and reinforcement.

143

SELF-ASSESSMENT
DISCUSSION QUESTIONS

1. What aspect of relating to people causes you the most anxiety?

2. Why do general social interaction skill problems cause anxiety?

3. How would you rate your general social interaction skills? What are your strong areas? Your weak areas?

4. Why is active listening such an important skill?

5. How would you define empathy? How is it different from sympathy?

6. What is meant by feedback? What happens when an individual becomes defensive about feedback?

7. How do you react to small talk? How good are you at it?

8. Why is small talk important?

9. Does making small talk create anxiety problems for you?

10. What is meant by nonverbal communication? Give some examples.

11. How is anxiety communicated nonverbally? What do you know about your own nonverbal behavior?

12. Why is the content of small talk less important than the message?

13. Do you have a genuine interest in others? Why or why not? Why is genuineness important?

14. Why do some people have interpersonal anxiety in groups?

15. Name and discuss some of the groups (formal and informal) to which you have belonged. Did the involvement make you anxious?

16. How would you define an intimate relationship?

17. Do you agree with the contention that all intimate relationships involve anxiety?

18. How do intimate relationships or the lack thereof cause anxiety?

19. How does one's sense of identity relate to one's capacity for intimacy?

20. How would you assess your own capacity for intimacy? What scares you about close relationships with people?

21. Do you currently have any intimate relationships? With males or females?

22. What is assertive behavior? How does it differ from passive or aggressive behavior?

23. Are you confident enough to accept the related responsibilites and consequences of assertiveness?

24. How does the failure to be assertive produce anxiety?

25. What are some of the reasons why people typically are not assertive? Why do you avoid being assertive?

26. When is it not appropriate to be assertive?

27. How can acceptance of social roles make assertive behavior difficult?

28. Why is risking anxiety related to a conflict better than being nonassertive?

ACTIVITIES

Activity 9.1 ACTIVE LISTENING

Purpose: This activity is designed to help you assess your listening skills and your ability to communicate empathic understanding.

Instructions. You need a partner for this activity. If you are working in a group, just pair up or if you are working by yourself, ask a friend to help you. Have your partner tell you about a problem or situation that has some personal meaning for him/her. Your job is to listen and to let the other person know that you understand what he/she is saying. If possible and with permission, you should audio-tape or video-tape the interaction. After about five minutes, stop the interaction, replay the tape, and have your friend give you feedback about your listening skills.

Before your partner gives feedback, discuss the concept of feedback. Helpful feedback has to be specific (describe behaviors, what was said, etc.): direct, constructive (not personally threatening—focus on what the person does most not on him/her as a person); and *reasonable* (most people can handle only a certain amount of negative feedback). Your friend (partner) should answer the following questions:

1. At what part of the interaction did you (the partner) feel that you were best understood?

2. What did the active listener say or do to communicate understanding and empathy?

3. How were you, the partner affected by the active listener's voice?

4. What specific verbal and nonverbal behaviors interfered with the active listener's communication of understanding?

5. How could the active listener have expressed greater empathy and understanding?

The listener should try several different interactions with different people so that you can gather a good sample of feedback about your listening skills. This feedback will provide you with a starting place to improve your listening skills. By learning to be a better listener your relationship skills will increase and you will feel more confident and less anxious in a variety of interpersonal situations.

Activity 9.2 BEGINNING CONVERSATIONS

Purpose: This activity will help you assess and improve your ability to begin relationships and to be effective in general social interaction.

Instructions: Make a list of three to five social interaction situations that frequently generate tension and anxiety for you (e.g., talking with someone you are interested in romantically, conversing at a party with someone you do not know, making conversation with neighbors, etc.).

After you have your list, write several opening lines for each situation. Then, with a partner, role play the particular situation. This practice may seem awkward in "acting out" the situation, but if you can improve your skills and lessen your anxiety in this role playing situation, you probably will feel less anxiety in the real situation. Choose a partner you trust and with whom you are comfortable. Stop after each interaction to ask for feedback from your partner; or if you role play in a small group, ask for comments from others in the group. This activity can help decrease the anxiety that comes from lack of skill in common social interactions. As you learn new ways to approach and to talk with individuals, you will become more comfortable and less anxious.

Activity 9.3 SUPPORT SYSTEMS

Purpose: To increase your understanding of your own personal support system.

Instructions: We all need support, particularly when we are feeling anxious and afraid. Look over the following anxiety situations and list two of your friends to whom you would consider for personal support.

1. Not getting along with your boss—excessive anxiety at work.

2. Afraid that your marriage is going sour.

3. Worried about flunking out of school.

4. Feeling much anxiety and tension with frequent tension headaches.

5. Increasing episodes of impotence/frigidity with your spouse/lover.

6. Worry about your children's behavior.

Think about/discuss the process you used to choose which friends with whom to talk. How would you be able to use their support? Would it decrease your anxiety?

Activity 9.4 INTIMACY

Purpose: This activity will help you explore the meaning of intimacy and of intimate relationships.

Instructions: List three intimate relationships that you have now or have had in the past. Remember that intimate relationships are not necessarily sexual. Now list several of the characteristics and/or important elements in each relationship. Also, write a few sentences explaining how this relationship developed into an intimate one. Finally, try to identify any fear/anxiety that was part of each of these relationships. What effect did it have? Did you overcome it? If you are working in a small group, compare your answers and discuss them.

This activity should help you explore the role of anxiety in intimate relationships and also the potential blocks that this anxiety can create.

Activity 9.5 ASSESSING SELF-DISCLOSURE

Purpose: This activity is designed to help you take a look at how much you typically disclose about yourself.

Instructions: Use the following scale to assess the self-disclosure statements that you make over the course of a few days. Carry a notebook with you and record as many statements as possible and then rate them according to the following scale.

Scale

Level 1—Superficial. No real self. Disclosure usually involves perfunctory social responses e.g., "How are you?" "Fine, and you?"

Level 2—Some self-disclosure. Some self-disclosure, but at a level that reveals little e.g., "How are you?" "OK, I guess, but work is getting me down."

Level 3—Significant self-disclosure. Usually within privare conversation where additional conversation is possible, e.g., "Tom, you look terrific. Come on in and have some coffee." "Thanks, Al. I am dying to tell somebody about this fantastic experience I had yesterday."

Level 4—Intimate self-disclosure. Sharing of something very personal, often a feeling or situation that makes one feel vulnerable e.g., "Carol, I have known you for a long time and I want you to know that your friendship is really important to me. I would really be hurt if you stopped liking me."

Look over your statements. Are you generally self-disclosing? Are you in situations where you can be self-disclosing? What prevented self-disclosure in situations where you did not reveal your true feelings? Did anxiety keep you from self-disclosure? Does anxiety often keep you from talking about yourself and your feelings?

If you are in a group, discuss your statements with the members.

Activity 9.6 ASSESSING ASSERTIVE BEHAVIOR

Purpose: To increase your ability to differentiate between your own assertive, aggressive, and passive responses.

Instructions: List ten situations in which you were either passive, assertive, or aggressive during the last week. Try to remember some of each kind. Write the response that you made and then write the two other possible types of responses.

Example. *A friend called and asked to borrow your car. This person frequently borrows your car but never puts in any gas.*

Actual Response (Passive)—Sure, go ahead.

Assertive Response—Yes, but put in some gas.

Aggressive response—No, damn it!—You never put in any gas.

Activity 9.7 BUILDING ASSERTIVE RESPONSES

Purpose: This activity will help develop your ability to be assertive and to recognize any passive or aggressive response tendencies.

Instructions: Work with a partner or a small group. Each person should write five statements representing situations in which they would find difficulty being assertive. The following are some examples:

1. Telling the boss at work that you do not agree with something.

2. Telling a friend that you cannot spend as much time in the future as you have been spending when talking to him/her on the telephone.

3. Telling your spouse or lover that something he/she is doing really makes you angry.

Write the statements on note cards and then exchange them with other group members. Each person should then write passive, aggressive, and assertive responses. Discuss differences of opinions. Then return the cards to the individual who wrote them and have that person role play an assertive response to each of his/her difficult situations.

BIBLIOGRAPHY

Alberti, R. & Emmons, M. *Your perfect right: A guide to assertive behavior.* San Luis Obispo, California: Impact, 1970.

Alberti, R. & Emmons, M. *Stand up, speak out, talk back!* New York: Pocket Books, 1975.

Carkhuff, R. *The art of helping.* Amhurst, Massachusetts: Human Resource Development Press, 1972.

Corey, G. *I never knew I had a choice.* Monterey, California: Brooks/Cole Publishing Co., 1978.

Egan, G. *You and me: The skills of communicating and relating to others.* Monterey, California: Brooks/Cole Publishing Co., 1977.

Erikson, E. *Childhood and society.* New York: Norton, 1964.

Gazda, G., Asbury, F., Balzer, F., Childers, W., & Walters, R. *Human relations development: A manual for educators* (2nd ed.). Boston: Allyn and Bacon, 1977.

Powell, J. *Why am I afraid to tell you who I am?* Niles, Illinois: Argus Communications, 1969.

Rogers, C. *On becoming a person.* Boston: Houghton Mifflin, 1961.

Wolpe, J. *The practice of behavior therapy* (2nd ed.). New York: PergamonPress, 1973.

Some people find that natural beauty helps them clarify their values.

Chapter 10

VALUES AND ANXIETY

Are your values clear and well defined? Or do you find yourself wondering what you really do value? The struggle to define values and to somehow live in accordance with one's values is one that most of us have in common. Often a considerable amount of anxiety is related to this struggle. Some anxiety about values is helpful, keeping your mind open to new ideas and forcing you to reevaluate your attitudes and beliefs regularly. On the other hand excessive anxiety about values can be immobilizing. If, for example, you can't make decisions because you just can't cope with the anxiety that choosing one value over another creates, your anxiety is clearly a problem.

For many people failing to act in concert with their true values creates excessive anxiety. This condition, called incongruence, is described in great detail by Carl Rogers (1961). Incongruence occurs when you are behaving as you feel you ought to behave, rather than in accordance with your beliefs and values. For example, if you believe that parents should spend time each day with their children, yet you seldom have time with your children because of your work, your behavior is incongruent with your values. The anxiety that results can be positive or negative. If it spurs you into working toward spending more time with your children, it is positive. If it makes you become angry and irritable at your children, it is negative and you probably will become even more anxious.

DEFINITION OF VALUES

Before discussing and studying ways to manage anxiety related values defining the term, value, will be helpful. Milton Rokeach (1973), a noted researcher of human values, used this definition:

> A *value* is an *enduring belief* that a specific mode of conduct or *end-state* of existence is personally or socially preferable to an opposite or converse mode of conduct or end-state of existence. A *value system* is an enduring organization of beliefs concerning preferable modes of conduct or end-states of existence along a continuum of relative importance (p. 5).

Several aspects of this definition deserve emphases:

1. A value is enduring. Generally speaking, a value has stability over time; however, values also must be viewed within a relativistic framework because they can change over time. Perry (1968 as a youngster you are taught that it is a sin to hurt others. This belief becomes an absolute value. Later, you discover that hurting others is acceptable in certain contexts (war, self-defense, etc.). Thus, you begin to understand different values in different contexts, and finally you begin the process of selecting personal values.

2. A value is a belief. A value is a belief that specifies a desirable or an appropriate way to behave, or an end-state to work toward. Usually an affective component exists in that you have feelings about the belief.

3. A value refers to a specific behavior or set of behaviors, or to an end-state or goal. A value can help you make a specific decision. You might decide, for example, not to attend an X-rated movie because of a value against sexual exploitation of women. Values also are related to long-term goals or states of existence. For instance, you might believe that women and men should be equal in a marriage relationship and, therefore, see a certain kind of marriage as an ideal end-state.

Complexities between values and anxiety management are less direct than complexities between physical relaxation and stress, or self-statements and stress. Four general aspects related to values dominate as potential anxiety problem areas. Consequently, improvement and growth in these aspects usually lead to lower levels of anxiety. These aspects include (1) value clarity, (2) changing and conflicting values, (3) conflicts between values and behavior, and (4) lack of commitment and involvement.

VALUE CLARITY

Poorly defined values cause anxiety in several ways. If one cannot identify his/her values, making life choices is very difficult. For example, the decision of what career to pursue cannot be made unless you know something about what is important and satisfying to you. Selecting a marriage partner is difficult unless you know what kind of relationship you want. Of course, many individuals are not totally certain about careers or marriages; but if some basis for choice does not exist, the chances for a successful career or marriage are doubtful.

Ambiguous values also make achieving an adequate sense of identity difficult. If you do not know how you feel about a number of issues, gaining any sense of self is difficult. In a social sense, lack of clear personal values also makes it difficult for others to know you. Like the color changing chameleon, confused values blend in with the environment and you really never communicate a personal identity.

Developing values and a value system is, of course, a life long process. Most of us find ourselves confused or uncertain at times. In a sense no one who is alive and growing ever has totally clear values; however, values can be clarified and movement made toward a more consistent belief system.

Conscious Awareness

One way to clarify values is to gain a conscious awareness of the values that you learned while you were maturing. People sometimes do not realize the extent that their past influences their present values. As a part of the natural process of maturing, the values we learned as children must be integrated with those we hold as adults. Sometimes this integration is difficult and anxiety producing because of the strong emotions related to values and because of the difficulty in identifying and separating childhood values from adult values.

If you have not given much thought to how and what values from childhood influence you, an effort to clarify these values may help you obtain a clearer picture of your current value conflicts and confusions. Following are a number of strategies you might use:

1. Think about significant people who influenced you. What values did they hold dear?

155

2. What values resulted from your religious training?

3. What values governed the rules for behavior in your family? What values underlie strongly forbidden behavior in your family?

4. What values did you react against as an adolescent?

5. What values were represented by your cultural/ethnic heritage?

6. Did you learn specific values from grandparents? Other relatives?

Value Clarification

Another approach to understanding values is called "Value Clarification." This method has been used primarily in small group, educational settings; and involves the use of structured activities to help people clarify their values and their valuing process (Kirschenbaum, 1977; Simon, Howe, & Kirschenbaum, 1972). Kirschenbaum (1977) suggested a method that emphasized five aspects of the valuing process: *thinking, feeling, choosing, communicating,* and *acting.* Growth in each area clarifies values and value related behavior.

Because the approach to value clarification developed by Simon et al. (1972) involves group interaction, some of the benefit of the approach is lost if you cannot perform the activities in a small group. The exercises suggested at the end of this chapter however can be performed individually or in groups.

Your Valuing Process

In addition to using various value clarification activities you can make progress in understanding and in clarifying your values if you confront your own valuing process. Ask yourself the following questions in each value process area:

1. *Thinking*

—Do you think critically and clearly about value questions?

—Do you identify alternatives in problem/decision situations?

—Are you able to think rationally even when you are emotionally involved in an issue?

2. *Feeling*

—Can you identify your feelings about value questions?

—Do you find descrepancies in your feelings about values?

—Do you consider your feelings about issues as well as your thoughts?

—Are you able to "prize and cherish" parts of yourself and the world?

3. *Choosing*

—Are you able to choose freely while understanding the pressures and consequences of decisions?

—Are you aware of your choice points?

—Can you make decisions?

4. *Communicating*

—Do you express your values to others?

—Can you be empathic and express understanding of someone else's point of view?

5. *Acting*

—Are you consistent in acting on your values?

—Do you have the skills necessary for achievement in your value areas?

CHANGING AND
CONFLICTING VALUES

Change and conflict of values often produce anxiety. The key to managing this anxiety is to understand and to accept the challenge or conflict as part of a creative developmental process.

Even people with well defined value systems are confronted with value change issues. These issues often emerge when one is confronted with new or different situations. A person may have strong values about certain sexual practices and then fall in love with someone with different and conflicting values. Or, as part of the general maturing process, a young person may find him/herself disagreeing with certain parental values. Accepting the difference is a bigger step than it seems, because it entails allowing others to think and behave differently. Allowing yourself to question a value that has been a pivotal one for you will not be easy. You can prevent unnecessary anxiety by allowing yourself the time and space to reconsider your beliefs. Instead of repressing your doubts, expose yourself to new ideas. Reconsider your values actively. Attend lectures, read books, talk to people.

For example you may believe that one should turn the other cheek and not fight back when people are aggressive. After you talk with several friends about a situation where a particular individual is taking advantage of you consistently, you also may begin to believe that every person has the right to defend him/herself and to be selfish. Thus, a value conflict begins to emerge. In time you may modify your "turn the other cheek value," or you may reaffirm it and decide that you don't have the right to defend yourself by being aggressive; however, if you don't allow yourself to actively reconsider values, the anxiety generated by the conflict probably will increase.

CONFLICTS BETWEEN VALUES AND BEHAVIOR

Authenticity is a word often used to describe people who are self-actualized (Maslow, 1968). These people are authentic, meaning that they behave according to their own beliefs and not according to other's expectations of them. In terms of general anxiety, the closer one comes to behaving in accordance with one's true values, the more inner peace one enjoys. Paradoxically, though, the process of working toward authenticity can generate considerable anxiety. This kind of anxiety which accompanies a quest for actualization is different in character than the anxiety that comes from refusing to pursue an integration of values and behavior. Value clarification is a key to this whole difficult actualization

158

process. This process requires one to somehow take the social, cultural, and parental influences and weave them into a set of values that are truly one's own.

Sometimes the decision to follow your values and really do what you want to do creates radical life style changes. Leaving a spouse, changing a career, or traveling to a far corner of the earth sometimes reflects the decision to change. Frequently, though, this kind of radical change is a desperate effort to break into a more satisfying way of living—without any real understanding of new values underlying that kind of life style.

If you discover differences between your values and your behavior, make a plan for changing your values, behavior, or both. Your behavior may take a radical change, or it may just mean a shift in emphasis. An interesting example of this kind of change often occurs with heart attack victims. Those who survive a first attack realize that their time on earth may be limited. This confrontation with mortality frequently produces significant life style changes. The person is forced, in a sense, to analyze his/her real values and to pursue them. The sense of urgency tends to break long established patterns of behavior and attitudes. This forced change may seem a bit grim, but take a minute to think about your own mortality. What if you only had a few years to live? Would you be doing what you are doing now or doing something very different?

Remember that to live authentically—in accordance with one's own values—is a life-long struggle. Everyone is trying to understand what they want and how to get it. Values play a very important role in the process, as does anxiety. Use your anxiety to promote your own personal growth. If you are always anxious and unclear about life decisions, use anxiety to seek more clarity. If you have a kind of gnawing discontent about your current life style, use this anxiety as impetus to search for new alternatives.

Lack of Commitment and Involvement

A special kind of fear and anxiety exists that prevents individuals from really engaging life. It is similar to the anxiety that prevents interpersonal commitment, but is more general in that it prevents commitment to just about everything. Risks of commitment are avoided at all costs. If you recognize some of this inability to commit yourself, consider the trade-off. By avoiding risk of commitment you are missing the feeling of excitement and exhilaration that can come from real involve-

159

ment. In a way, you are paying a high price for avoiding anxiety. By successfully applying anxiety management techniques however you may be able to overcome some of your fears and be able to risk involvement. If, for example, you manage your interpersonal anxiety better, you will have a greater sense of confidence with people and therefore be able to risk involvement. Or, if you are able to combat irrational needs to be perfect, you may be able to try behaviors that you cannot perform perfectly.

SUMMARY

1. Everyone experiences anxiety related to values. For some, the anxiety coming from unclear or confused values creates difficulty in making life decisions. For others, anxiety comes from not living in accordance with personal values.

2. A basic definition of values includes these three elements: (a) a value is enduring, (b) a value is a belief, and (c) a value refers to a specific behavior or set of behaviors or to a desired end-state or goal.

3. To explore values and anxiety focusing on these four areas is useful: (a) value clarity, (b) changing and conflicting values, (c) conflicts between values and behavior, and (d) lack of commitment and involvement.

4. Unclear and confused values make decisions difficult. This difficulty often creates anxiety.

5. One strategy for clarifying your current values is to seek a better understanding of how your values developed.

6. An examination of parental, cultural, social, and other value influences may help you integrate your current values with those brought from your past.

7. Value clarification, which involves participating in a variety of activities designed to facilitate viewing and identifying values, can help you clarify your values.

8. Value clarification theorists have defined the valuing process as including thinking, feeling, choosing, communicating, and acting.

9. By considering and discussing your own valuing process in the above mentioned areas, you can begin to clarify your valuing processes.

10. Conflicting and changing values often cause anxiety.

11. Much of this kind of anxiety is generated as part of a reaction against change.

12. Although values are defined as enduring, they do change and develop. An acceptance of this growth-oriented approach can help in the struggle with new and conflicting values.

13. Part of this acceptance of change also involves the acceptance of value differences. This acceptance of value differences requires that one move past the belief that issues are always either right or wrong.

14. Few individuals are at a point in life where their behavior is totally in concert with their values and beliefs.

15. When people feel locked in to a life style that is not really what they want, they sometimes take radical action, like leaving a spouse, or leaving a career to seek a closer accomodation to their values.

16. A more gradual change process is possible also. The first step involves clarifying values in question.

17. The next step is a plan for change that leads to a more authentic life style.

18. A special kind of avoidance anxiety prevents some people from generally committing themselves to anything.

SELF-ASSESSMENT
DISCUSSION QUESTIONS

1. How can value-related issues cause anxiety?

2. What are the three parts of Rokeach's value definition? Do you agree with this definition?

3. How do ambigious or confused values create anxiety?

4. What is value clarification? How would you describe your progress in understanding and defining your values?

5. Why is it useful to understand something about the values that you have internalized from the past?

6. What are the five parts of the valuing process?

7. Do you agree that communicating is an essential element? Does one have to communicate one's values to others?

8. How do feelings and emotions relate to the valuing process?

9. Do feelings play an important role in your valuing process?

10. Give an example of how conflicting values cause anxiety. Can you think of an example from your own life?

11. What is meant by accepting the validity of value differences?

12. If values, by definition, are enduring, how can one reconcile value change?

13. What role does anxiety play in value conflict and change?

14. What is meant by incongruence?

15. What happens to you when you discover that you are involved in activities that you do not value?

16. Do you agree that the struggle toward authenticity is life long?

17. When do you feel most authentic and in tune with your values?

18. How can anxiety prevent lack of commitment and risk taking?

19. Is lack of commitment and involvement a problem for you?

ADDITIONAL ACTIVITIES

Many activities are available that can help you clarify unclear and conflicting values and achieve a better understanding of how much your behavior reflects your values. A few activities that have specific relevance to the relationship between anxiety and values are suggested.

Activity 10.1 VALUE PRIORITIES

Purpose: The purpose of this activity is to help you identify and consider your value priorities. This list is not exclusive, so add other values that figure prominently in your value system.

Instructions: Prioritize the following list of values in order of their importance to you. If you are participating working in a group, compare your order with others in the group and discuss how you arrived at your decisions. After you have completed your priority list, repeat the process and prioritize the items as you think you would have five years ago. Any changes? Can you predict changes five years in the future? Try to identify a behavior related to each value. Do your behaviors seem to jive with your priorities?

Value List

Prosperity (being comfortable materially)

Achievement (accomplishing something important and lasting)

Personal Happiness (being content and generally happy)

Morality (living up to a high standard of personal morality)

Power (being influential)

Spirituality (having a satisfying spiritual life)

Self-esteem (positive feelings about self)

163

Status (having others admire and respect you)

Friendship (being close to others)

Independence (ability to make your own decisions)

Love (intimacy with spouse, lover, or family)

Charity (giving to others less fortunate)

Learning (gaining new knowledge)

Serenity (feeling calm and peaceful)

This activity can help you focus on value confusion and value conflict. Look for conflicting values that seem to occur frequently. Also, evaluate your behavior and how it corresponds to your values. Can you identify anxiety related to your not behaving in accordance with your values?

Activity 10.2 VALUE DEVELOPMENT

Purpose: This activity is designed to get you to examine your past, present, and future values. By remembering past events and related values, you can reflect upon the growth of your values; and by designating future ways of actualizing other values, you will gain insight into the relationship between values and behavior.

Instructions: Use a wide piece of paper (tape a couple of standard size sheets together if necessary) and draw a horizontal line from left to right. Place a point on the far left and label it "birth" and place a point on the far right and label it "death." Put in a point for the "present" somewhere in the middle. Mark in two or three events on your life line that have had a significant influence on your life. How have these events effected the development of your value system? Next mark in two or three points in the future representing events that you would like to have happen. How do these events represent your current and developing value system? By understanding more about the development of your value system, you can get a clearer picture of your value development and related anxiety.

Activity 10.3 CHOOSING VALUES

Purpose: This activity forces you to confront value choices and conflicts.

Instructions: Examine the following list of choices and try to decide which word is more like you. If you are participating in a group, pair up with someone, compare your answers, discuss reasons for your choice, and identify values underlying your choices. If you are not participating in a group, make your choices and then discuss them with a friend. See if the friend would have guessed the same choices that you made for yourself. This discussion will give you some idea of how your outward behavior and appearance reflect your values.

Circle one.

1. Country   City

2. Red   Blue

3. Quiet   Talkative

4. Aggressive   Passive

5. Past   Present

6. Feeling   Thinking

7. Order   Flexibility

8. Knowledge   Power

9. Car   Bicycle

10. Leader   Follower

11. Candy   Vegetable

12. Football   Track

13. Dirt   Cement

14. English   Math

15. Play   Work

Activity 10.4 CONFLICTING VALUES

Purpose: To highlight personal value conflicts and ways to cope with the resulting anxiety.

Instructions: List two or three value related conflicts that you are currently experiencing. After you list each conflict try to isolate two words that represent the conflict. (see the following examples)

Example 1. Conflict between wanting free time to spend with family or friends and wanting to excel in your career by working on weekends. *freedom* vs. *achievement*

Example 2. Conflict between wanting to settle down and have a serious relationship and wanting to be free to have a number of different relationships. *intimacy* vs. *freedom*

Example 3. Wanting to be supportive and spend time with a friend who is having problems and wanting to go away to the beach with another friend. *responsibility* vs. *pleasure*

Discuss your conflicts with a friend or small group. Indicate how you usually cope with anxiety related to each conflict and acquire other suggestions and ideas if possible.

Activity 10.5 VALUES AND BEHAVIOR

Purpose: This activity is designed to help participants answer the question, "Am I really getting what I want out of life?" It helps you take a look at those things that you really prize and to determine whether or not you are actually doing them.

Instructions: Make a list of fifteen activities that you really enjoy doing, leave a very wide margin on the left side of your list. The list might include activities such as eating a chocolate ice cream cone, doing volunteer work, or helping a needy family. After you have completed your list, make five columns on the left side. Fill in the following information in each column next to each of the fifteen activities in your list!

Column 1—Put a "M" next to each item that costs more than $1.

Column 2—Put the number of times you have done the activity in the last two weeks.

Column 3—Put an "S" next to the activities that can be done spontaneously and a "P" next to the ones that must be planned.

Column 4—Put an "O" next to activities that you do with others and an "I" next to those you do alone.

Column 5—Classify the activity as either Physical, Intellectual, or Social by putting "P","I" or "S" in column 5.

After you have completed coding your choices, take a good look at what you have written. Do you notice any discrepancies between what you say and what you do? How do you account for these descrepancies? What conclusions can you make about your values from this activity? If you are working alone, have a good friend look over your list and discuss it with you. Does it match their perceptions of you? If you are working in a group, divide into diads and discuss your choices, why you made these choices, and what they mean to you. Or have different people put their list on a chalkboard or large piece of newsprint and discuss their choices and their implications. Personal items can be left out of group discussion if desired. This activity focuses strongly on the relationship of values to behavior. You should gain a good idea of just how much your behavior matches your values. If you find descrepancies, try to identify how these discrepancies can cause anxiety. Are there particular times when you want to do some of the activities you listed and cannot?

A number of additional value clarification activities are contain in *Values Clarification: A Handbook of Practical Strategies for Teachers and Students* by S. B. Simon, New York: Hart Publishing Co., 1972.

BIBLIOGRAPHY

Kirschenbaum, H. *Advanced value clarification.* La Jolle, California: University Associates, 1977.

Maslow, A. *Toward a psychology of being* (2nd. ed.). New York: Van Nostrand Reinhold, 1968.

Perry, W. *Forms of intellectual and ethical development in the college years.* New York: Holt, Reinhart, and Winston, 1968.

Rogers, C. *On becoming a person.* Boston: Houghton Mifflin Co., 1961.

Rokeach, M. *The nature of human values.* New York: The Free Press, 1973.

Simon, S. B., Howe, L. W., & Kirschenbaum, H. *Values clarification: A handbook of practical strategies for teachers and students.* New York: Hart Publishing Co., 1972.

Managing time related anxiety sometimes means taking time for new kinds of relaxation.

Chapter 11

TIME AND ANXIETY

Think about time for a moment. What does it mean for an individual? Everyone has time, at least within the limits of their life (and perhaps thereafter, depending upon their religious beliefs). If you live to be 70 years old, you have a total of about 613,200 hours to use. That number seems immense, yet we often feel that there are just not enough hours in each day. Time seems scarce, and in this society one often has to decide priorities for how to use time.

This sense of scarcity and the apparent need for more hours has created what Friedman and Rosenman (1973) called the "hurry sickness." This sickness is really a disease of anxiety. They described people who have a sense of *chronic time urgency* as having Type A behavior. In many ways, hurry sickness is the result of industrialized society. Nowotny (1975, p. 329), in an article presented at the second conference of the International Study of Time, suggested that "...time will be accorded value whenever it comes to be considered rare from the point of view of the individual." In other words, the less time one has, the more valued it becomes. The anxiety related to hurry sickness may be a result of one's perception of the scarcity of time.

Clearly, one's perceptions of time and the way one uses time can create anxiety. Few people escape the tense feeling that comes when time seems to run out. The breathless friend who yells, "Sorry, I am running late . . ., can't stop," or the business associate who comes in ten minutes late and is visibly flustered by being behind schedule, are but two examples of a very common phenomena.

169

Your personality and the way you view the world also effect your attitudes toward time and your use of time. For example, do you see unexpected events as delays that get in the way of what you have planned or as opportunities that allow you to spontaneously pursue some new topic or direction. Your view can greatly effect the degree of anxiety that is produced.

In this chapter three approaches to the management of time-related anxiety are presented. The first approach focuses on the perception of time as a scarce commodity. The Type A personality/behavior profile will be presented with suggestions for how you can modify excessive anxiety related to Type A behavior. The second approach provides an opportunity to examine personality variables that effect the way you use and perceive time. The awareness that you gain will help you modify and work on time uses and perceptions that cause excessive anxiety. The third approach concerns your *use* of time. The importance of effective time management skills will be examined along with suggestions for effective time management systems.

TYPE A BEHAVIOR

Doctors Friedman and Rosenman (1973) have identified one way of viewing relationship between personality and time-related anxiety. In their views, a specific cluster of behaviors and related personality traits exist in people whom they call Type A. People who are Type A tend to be more anxious and prone to heart disease. Their perception of time as a *scarce* commodity and their quest to outrun the clock is probably the central characteristic of Type A behavior: ". . . Type A behavior pattern is an action-emotion complex that can be observed in any person who is *aggressively* involved in *chronic,* incessant struggle to achieve more and more in less and less time" (Friedman & Rosenman, 1973, p. 67). From their research they have concluded that Type A behavior is the number one cause of heart disease.

Type B behavior is the opposite of Type A. Type B's are not driven to accomplish more and more. They are less aggressive, less competitive, and seem to be generally more relaxed. According to Friedman and Rosenman (1973), over 50 percent of the urban Americans that they have evaluated are in the Type A category and about 40 percent are Type B.

Time-related anxiety is clearly a major part of Type A pattern. The chronic sense of time urgency and competitiveness keep this kind of per-

170

son on edge most of the time. He/she can never really relax because there are more things to do and more people with whom to compete. Type A Behavior Inventory, designed to help you identify how many Type A behaviors and attitudes you generally possess, is provided as Table ll.l.

Activity 11.1 ASSESSING TYPE A BEHAVIOR

Purpose: To rate the frequency of Type A behaviors and attitudes.

Instructions: Complete the Type A Behavior Inventory presented in Table ll.l. Use the pronoun "I" in front of each behavior and then using the Rating Scale provided rate the frequency for which the statement is true for you.

Determine the extent of your Type A behavior by using the Scoring Scale provided at the end of the Inventory.

Table 11.1

Type A Behavior Inventory*

Rating Scale: For each behavior listed assign the value to indicate the frequency with which the behavior occurs.

2 = Frequently
1 = Sometimes
0 = Almost Never

1. *Verbally aggressive/impatient*

_____Explosively accentuate key words.

_____Increase the speed of the last few words of sentence.

*NOTE: This inventory is based on the description of Type A behavior in R.M. Friedman and R.H. Rosenman, *Type A Behavior and Your Heart,* New York: Knopf, 1974.

Table 11.1 Continued

2. *Generally hurried*

   _____Move, walk and eat rapidly.

3. *Impatient with the rate of most things*

   _____Try to hurry speech of others.

   _____Say yes, yes or uh huh trying to urge others to talk faster.

   _____Finish sentences for others.

   _____Get unduly irritated in slow traffic.

   _____Become unnerved by having to wait in line.

   _____Become intolerable when watching others work more slowly than normally done by self.

   _____Impatient with routine tasks (washing clothes, writing checks, etc.).

   _____Hurry reading (skip to summaries).

4. *Try to do several things simultaneously*

   _____Try to think or do two or more things simultaneously.

   _____Think about one thing when trying to attend to another.

5. *Self-preoccupation*

   _____Try to steer conversations around to your own interests.

   _____Pretend to listen but remain preoccupied with your own thoughts.

172

Table 11.1 continued

6. *Relaxation difficulties*

   _____Feel vague guilt feelings when relaxing.

7. *Poor observer-miss interesting and beautiful things in your life*

   _____Move quickly without stopping to enjoy flowers, trees, etc.

   _____Cannot recall things previously seen in various places.

8. *Preoccupied with getting rather than being*

   _____Strive for material possessions.

   _____Go about daily activities without reflecting.

9. *Chronic time urgency*

   _____Feel an almost constant need for more time in the schedule.

   _____Have trouble with unforeseen contingencies.

10. *Aggressive toward other Type A's*

    _____Argue or frequently confront people who behave in ways similar to self.

    _____Feel little compassion for others with "hurry sickness."

11. *Characteristic gestures or tics*

    _____Clench fist or bang your hand during conversation.

    _____Clench jaw, grind teeth, or have spasmodical tic.

Table 11.1 continued

12. *Believe that success is related to speed*

_____Must compete and do things faster.

_____Seem afraid to slow down (possess an urge to stay ahead of others).

13. *Emphasis on numbers*

_____Translate activities into numbers (how many, how much).

_____Emphasize *quantity* rather than *quality.*

Scoring: This instrument is not scientifically validated; however, you can obtain a rough idea of the extend of your own Type A behavior by adding your scores and comparing to the following scale.

        50 - 60 = Type A
        30 - 49 = A number of Type A characteristics
        10 - 29 = Some Type A behaviors
        0 - 9 = Few Type A behaviors, more likely a Type B individual

Comments Following Completion of Type A Behavior Inventory. Friedman and Rosenman (1973) believed that Type A behavior can be changed and that attempting to change this pattern is worthwhile anytime in life. Change is difficult because many Type A people delude themselves into thinking that they will be able to escape negative effects. It cannot happen to them. If you are one of these people trying to cling to Type A behaviors by rationalizing away the negative effects—beware!! Consider what you are giving up—the chance for a more relaxed, longer, and probably more fulfilling life.

Changing Type A Behavior

Change from Type A behavior to Type B is possible, but but you have to want to change. To convince yourself that it's just your personality and that you can't really do anything about your Type A behavior is easy to do. This belief is just not true. Many techniques that you are learning from this book will help you modify your Type A behavior, but you really have to make a commitment to some basic life style changes. This doesn't necessarily mean that you have to give up the good life or that you have to become a beach bum. In many ways decreasing Type A behavior will unlock new ways for you to be creative and productive.

Following are some ways that you can work toward elimination of Type A behavior.

1. *Take an honest look at yourself.* The first step in any personal change process is self-awareness. To take an honest look at how you are living your life is difficult. It is particularly difficult for Type A people because they never let themselves get enough distance to see what is really happening to them. Frequently a major life event like death or divorce seems to be necessary to jolt them into looking at themselves. The Type A behavior inventory should have helped you assess your Type A behavior. If you see Type A behaviors in yourself, try to explore them. Ask your close friends and relatives if they see these kinds of behaviors in you. Make a copy of the Type A inventory, look at it periodically to see if you are engaging in Type A behavior.

2. *Clarify your values.* Are you doing what you really want to do? Take time out to think about what is important to you. The chapter on values should have helped you with this process. People with Type A behavior are often so busy with trivia that they loose track of many of life's gifts. Fathers see their children grown and suddenly realize that they've been too busy really to enjoy being a parent. Attending the funeral of their mother or father grown children realize that they have been too busy over the years to really enjoy time with their parents. Type A behavior can rob you of many of the humane, precious parts of life. Many of these moments require a sense of relaxation and openness that you just can't experience when rushing from one activity to the next.

Try to shed some of your materialism. We are all in a culture that encourages us to spend and acquire goods. In many ways Type A people are caught up in a competitive, materialistic struggle—if you see this in yourself, think about the consequences. Is this frantic race worth the effort? Is it worth the anxiety and lower life expectancy that it can produce? Friedman and Roseman (1973) capture the essence of the real question, "What apart from the external clutter of my everyday living should be the essence of my life?" (p. 191).

3. *Don't compete unnecessarily.* Competition may be necessary at times, but you don't have to become obsessed with it. Type A people often feel someone just one step behind them with whom they are always competing. Is a lifelong sense of competition worth the potential rewards? It may get you more money or a better job, but consider the things you might miss. Competition is another one of the dominant cultural values that we need to call into question.

4. *Readjust your attitudes toward time.* Somehow we all become a slave to the clock at one time or other. If you are a Type A, your life may be largely governed by the need to beat the clock. Experiment with giving less emphasis to time. When you go on vacation try living without clocks, see if you can structure your life without time. You'll find it difficult at first, but you may get some insight into how time is enslaving you.

A classic sign of Type A behavior is the need to fill all your time with productive activities. If you have this problem, you probably feel guilty anytime that you relax and take time out to do nothing. This may mean that somehow you've learned that you need to be producing every moment. In a sense you are overemphasizing outcome rather than process. Existing and relaxing without any goal or end point has value. If this is difficult to believe, then you probably are suffering from a major Type A symptom.

One way to challenge a dysfunctional attitude toward time (the attitude previously described dysfunctional) is to spend some time with someone who isn't a slave to time. See what not to worry about what you have to do during the next hour is like. Granted, you do not want to become totally oblivious to time, but room to loosen up exists.

5. *Create peaceful surroundings for yourself.* This anxiety reducing principle includes physical and psychological surroundings. Try to create space where you can retreat regularly and relax. If you have children or live with others, find a place to which you can retreat. Perhaps you will have to work with the other people around you to allow you time and

space for quiet. Examine seriously your mode of socializing and recreation. Is it hectic? If you don't have people and things that help you relax, then you need to add some relaxing activities and people. What about your career? Do you work in an environment where the boss thinks that the best way to manage people is to keep them anxious and overcome with work tasks? If this is the case, you might want to consider changing jobs. Or, maybe you are the boss: Take a look at how you operate. Do you get too involved with too many details? Are you able to delegate enough to get time away from work? See what you can do to create a more relaxed and peaceful environment for yourself. In the long run, you and your employees will be more productive.

6. *Identify and modify specific Type A behaviors.* In addition to awareness and attitudinal change, you should try to change behavior that is clearly Type A. If, for example, you consistently work on Saturday and Sunday, begin to substitute recreational activities for work. Approach the change gradually. Start by cutting down your work time by a few hours each week. Remember that to change behavior you really have to make a commitment to change.

7. *Explore the meaning of life in new ways.* Type A people frequently loose their perspective on life. They see everything from a very narrow perspective. A multitude of ways exist to expand your perspective. A walk in the woods will do it for some people, others thrive on listening to music that inspires them. Be creative and take time for something that you have always wanted to try.

ANXIETY AND PERSONALITY

One way of considering how your personality interacts with your experience of time-related anxiety is through Carl Jung's (1923) system of personality preferences and types. Although content space is too limited to explain Jung's entire system, you should be able to learn enough from the following abbreviated version to get an idea of how some of your personality preferences effect your use and perception of time. Jung's (1923) theory of personality types was first operationalized in the Myers-Briggs Type Indicator (1962). This instrument is available only from certified counselors or psychologists; however, the Keirsey Temperment Sorter (1978) can be used to gain a general idea of your type preferences. The Temperment Sorter is an integral part of Activity 11.2.

Activity 11.2 PERSONALITY TYPE PREFERENCES

Purpose: To analyze personal preferences in the four areas.

Instructions: Use Table 11.2, Keirsey Temperment Sorter, to gain a general idea of your personality type preference. Complete the Sorter using Table 11.3, Answer Sheet, provided.

After you complete the Sorter, determine your score by using the "Scoring Directions" in Table 11.3 before you continue reading the remaining part of this chapter.

Table 11.2

Keirsey Temperament Sorter

Place a check in the appropriate box on the answer sheet, Table 11.3, that follows this Sorter. The answer sheet can be torn out or you can use it to make your own answer sheet.

The Keirsey Temperament Sorter*

1. At a party do you
    (a) interact with many, including strangers
    (b) interact with a few, known to you

2. Are you more
    (a) realistic than speculative
    (b) speculative than realistic

3. Is it worse to
    (a) have your "head in the clouds"
    (b) be "in a rut"

4. Are you more impressed by
    (a) principles   (b) emotions

---

*From *Please Understand Me: An Essay on Temperament Styles* by D. Keirsey and M. Bates, Del Mar, California: Promethean Books, Inc., 1978, pp. 5-10. Reprinted with permission.

Table 11.2 Continued

5. **Are you more drawn toward the**
   (a) convincing   (b) touching

6. **Do you prefer to work**
   (a) to deadlines   (b) just "whenever"

7. **Do you tend to choose**
   (a) rather carefully   (b) somewhat impulsively

8. **At parties do you**
   (a) stay late, with increasing energy
   (b) leave early, with decreased energy

9. **Are you more attracted to**
   (a) sensible people   (b) imaginative people

10. **Are you more interested in**
    (a) what is actual   (b) what is possible

11. **In judging others are you more swayed by**
    (a) laws than circumstances
    (b) circumstances than laws

12. **In approaching others is your inclination to be somewhat**
    (a) objective   (b) personal

13. **Are you more**
    (a) punctual   (b) leisurely

14. **Does it bother you more having things**
    (a) incomplete   (b) completed

15. **In your social groups do you**
    (a) keep abreast of other's happenings
    (b) get behind on the news

16. **In doing ordinary things are you more likely to**
    (a) do it the usual way   (b) do it your own way

Table 11.2 Continued

17. **Writers should**
    (a) "say what they mean and mean what they say"
    (b) express things more by use of analogy

18. **Which appeals to you more**
    (a) consistency of thought
    (b) harmonious human relationships

19. **Are you more comfortable in making**
    (a) logical judgments   (b) value judgments

20. **Do you want things**
    (a) settled and decided   (b) unsettled and undecided

21. **Would you say you are more**
    (a) serious and determined   (b) easy-going

22. **In phoning do you**
    (a) rarely question that it will all be said
    (b) rehearse what you'll say

23. **Facts**
    (a) "speak for themselves"
    (b) illustrate principles

24. **Are visionaries**
    (a) somewhat annoying
    (b) rather fascinating

25. **Are you more often**
    (a) a cool-headed person   (b) a warm-hearted person

26. **Is it worse to be**
    (a) unjust   (b) merciless

27. **Should one usually let events occur**
    (a) by careful selection and choice
    (b) randomly and by chance

28. **Do you feel better about**
    (a) having purchased   (b) having the option to buy

Table 11.2 Continued

29. In company do you
    (a) initiate conversation   (b) wait to be approached

30. Common sense is
    (a) rarely questionable   (b) frequently questionable

31. Children often do not
    (a) make themselves useful enough
    (b) exercise their fantasy enough

32. In making decisions do you feel more comfortable with
    (a) standards   (b) feelings

33. Are you more
    (a) firm than gentle   (b) gentle than firm

34. Which is more admirable:
    (a) the ability to organize and be methodical
    (b) the ability to adapt and make do

35. Do you put more value on the
    (a) definite   (b) open-ended

36. Does new and non-routine interaction with others
    (a) stimulate and energize you
    (b) tax your reserves

37. Are you more frequently
    (a) a practical sort of person
    (b) a fanciful sort of person

38. Are you more likely to
    (a) see how others are useful
    (b) see how others see

39. Which is more satisfying:
    (a) to discuss an issue thoroughly
    (b) to arrive at agreement on an issue

40. Which rules you more:
    (a) your head   (b) your heart

Table 11.2 Continued

41. Are you more comfortable with work that is
    (a) contracted   (b) done on a casual basis

42. Do you tend to look for
    (a) the orderly   (b) whatever turns up

43. Do you prefer
    (a) many friends with brief contact
    (b) a few friends with more lengthy contact

44. Do you go more by
    (a) facts   (b) principles

45. Are you more interested in
    (a) production and distribution
    (b) design and research

46. Which is more of a compliment:
    (a) "There is a very logical person."
    (b) "There is a very sentimental person."

47. Do you value in yourself more that you are
    (a) unwavering   (b) devoted

48. Do you more often prefer the
    (a) final and unalterable statement
    (b) tentative and preliminary statement

49. Are you more comfortable
    (a) after a decision   (b) before a decision

50. Do you
    (a) speak easily and at length with strangers
    (b) find little to say to strangers

51. Are you more likely to trust your
    (a) experience   (b) hunch

52. Do you feel
    (a) more practical than ingenious
    (b) more ingenious than practical

Table 11.2 Continued

53. **Which person is more to be complimented: one of**
    (a) clear reason   (b) strong feeling

54. **Are you inclined more to be**
    (a) fair-minded   (b) sympathetic

55. **Is it preferable mostly to**
    (a) make sure things are arranged
    (b) just let things happen

56. **In relationships should most things be**
    (a) renegotiable
    (b) random and circumstantial

57. **When the phone rings do you**
    (a) hasten to get to it first
    (b) hope someone else will answer

58. **Do you prize more in yourself**
    (a) a strong sense of reality   (b) a vivid imagination

59. **Are you drawn more to**
    (a) fundamentals   (b) overtones

60. **Which seems the greater error:**
    (a) to be too passionate   (b) to be too objective

61. **Do you see yourself as basically**
    (a) hard-headed   (b) soft-hearted

62. **Which situation appeals to you more:**
    (a) the structured and scheduled
    (b) the unstructured and the unscheduled

63. **Are you a person that is more**
    (a) routinized than whimsical
    (b) whimsical than routinized

64. **Are you more inclined to be**
    (a) easy to approach   (b) somewhat reserved

Table 11.2 Continued

---

65. In writings do you prefer
   (a) the more literal   (b) the more figurative

66. Is it harder for you to
   (a) identify with others   (b) utilize others

67. Which do you wish more for yourself:
   (a) clarity of reason   (b) strength of compassion

68. Which is the greater fault:
   (a) being indiscriminate   (b) being critical

69. Do you prefer the
   (a) planned event   (b) unplanned event

70. Do you tend to be more
   (a) deliberate than spontaneous
   (b) spontaneous than deliberate

Table 11.3
Answer Sheet for Keirsy Temperament Sorter*

	a	b		a	b		a	b		a	b		a	b		a	b		a	b
1			2			3			4			5			6			7		
8			9			10			11			12			13			14		
15			16			17			18			19			20			21		
22			23			24			25			26			27			28		
29			30			31			32			33			34			35		
36			37			38			39			40			41			42		
43			44			45			46			47			48			49		
50			51			52			53			54			55			56		
57			58			59			60			61			62			63		
64			65			66			67			68			69			70		

1   2   3   4   3   4   5   6   5   6   7   8   7   8

1   2   3   4   5   6   7   8

    E   I   S   N   T   F   J   P

Scoring Directions*

1. Add down so that the total number of "a" answers is written in the box at the bottom each column. Do the same for the "b" answers you have checked. Each of the 14 boxes should have a number in it.

---

*From *Please Understand Me: An Essay on Temperament Styles* by D. Keirsey and M. Bates, Del Mar, California: Promethean Books, Inc., 1978, pp. 11-12. Reprinted with permission.

Table 11.3 Continued

---

2. Transfer the number in box No. 1 of the answer sheet to box No. 1 below the answer sheet. Do this for box No. 2 as well. Note, however, that you have two numbers for boxes 3 through 8. Bring down the first number for each box beneath the second, as indicated by the arrows. Now add all the pairs of numbers and enter the total in the boxes below the answer sheet, so each box has only one number.

3. Now you have four pairs of numbers. Circle the letter below the larger number of each pair. If the two numbers of any pair are equal, then circle neither, but put a large X below them and circle it.

Comments For Table 11.3. The letter you have circled as Step 3 in Scoring Directions is your preference. You should have four letters circled. Each circled letter indicates a preference for a particular personality function, unless you have a tied score and if that is the case you probably don't have a very decisive preference on that particular function.

The following explanation of eight personality types related to functions and preferences you marked on Keirsey Temperment Sorter, Tables 11.2 and 11.3 will help you better understand your perception and use of time. Suggestions for specific types of people should be useful in your attempts to decrease excessive time-related anxiety.

Extroversion (E) Versus Introversion (I)

Extroverts (E) tend to be more sociable, they get their energy from other people and can spend long periods of time with others. Introverts (I) need more time alone. They are less sociable and need more privacy. Introverts can spend long periods of time by themselves and often are engaged in self-reflection in their own private world.

Introverts and Extroverts tend to view time from different perspectives. An Extrovert views time more in relationship to other people. Because Extroverts are more people-oriented, they sometimes have trouble in situations where they cannot have access to people. An Extrovert who tries to bury him/herself in the library all day probably will become tense unless he/she can take some "people breaks." An Introvert on the other hand, will start to feel anxious if too much time is spent around people. An Introvert also is more likely to loose track of time during periods when he/she is engrossed in self-reflection. The value of time will be seen differently by people with these two preferences. Introverts will value their personal time alone more while Extroverts will tend to value time structured with people. Each will experience anxiety if their kind of time is not available.

An understanding and acceptance of your particular preferences will help you manage anxiety by organizing your life to allow for preferences. Introverts need to structure time so as to have blocks of time to be alone in their daily schedule. This structuring may mean communicating this need to spouses, lovers, friends, and parents. This communication may be difficult because Introverts often feel and believe that others feel that their need for private time is not legitimate. Generally, people do not encourage a person to spend time alone.

Time-related anxiety for Extroverts is more often a result of their trouble with spending too much time talking to people. Suddenly, the day is over and they have not achieved their goals. The anxiety created by this lack of achievement can accelerate rapidly if important job or life tasks are not accomplished. Better assertiveness skills may be necessary and clear goals and rewards may be helpful to encourage goal-directed activity.

Intuition (N) Versus Sensing (S)

This preference describes how one perceives the world. Individuals who prefer Sensing (S) acquire information directly through the senses. They tend to see, hear, smell, feel, and taste things directly. They are practical, down to earth people who are attuned to reality. They are more interested in types of work that are practical and applied. On the other hand people who prefer Intuition (N) absorb information indirectly as well as directly. They are more apt to see possibilities as well as reality. They are more imaginative, more comfortable with abstraction, and probably more creative, but they may have trouble getting things done. They would prefer to have ideas and have someone else implement them.

People who prefer Sensing (S) consider time in specific terms. They tend to use it to implement functional tasks in a practical manner. They control time by compartmentalizing it and using it for specific projects or activities. People who prefer Intuition (N) more easily lose track of time

187

because they are less imprisoned by external time cues. They do not notice the clock, particularly if they are thinking about an idea and involved in a project. Time controlling and scheduling may be less important to them. They may be even more oblivious to external time cues if they also are Introverts (I) and internally oriented much of the time. Their orientation is more often toward the future where time is more elusive.

If you prefer Intuition (N) and experience anxiety related to this difficulty in time awareness, you may want to teach yourself to pay more attention to external time clues. Use your creativity to develop ways of being more specific about your own time requirements. A number of useful suggestions will be presented in the section on Time Management Skills.

If you prefer Sensing (S), you probably experience anxiety when the use of time is unspecified. If you receive an assignment that is open ended with few perimeters, you will probably become anxious unless you can somehow organize the task into manageable time units. Your best anxiety management approach probably is to learn how to focus energy on setting your own time perimetors.

An understanding of how Intuitor-Sensor differences can affect perceptions of time will help you minimize potential conflict and anxiety. Take, for example, a boss who strongly prefers Intuition (N). When he gives assignments to his employees, often he is vague and nonspecific. If he happens to be giving directions to an employee who is a strong Sensor, (S) the vagueness and nonspecificity is apt to be very difficult for the employee. A person who prefers Sensing (S) will expect concrete directions. If you are either the boss or the employee, an understanding of these differences will help you work toward better communication. If you are the employee, you can ask for more structure, realizing that you may not get as much as you like. Or, if you are the boss, you can attempt to be more specific even though it isn't your natural style.

Thinking (T) and Feeling (F)

People who prefer Thinking (T) usually make their decisions based upon an objective, rational analysis of information, while people who prefer Feeling (F) make decisions based upon personal feelings and values. Their decisions are not necessarily logical or rational. Remember that although one may *prefer* Thinking or Feeling everyone has the ability to use *both* Thinking and Feeling. People who prefer Feeling consider

188

time from a value perspective. When they feel strongly about something, they usually will devote time to it, often at the expense of something else about which they feel less strongly. People who prefer Thinking, on the other hand, probably are more able to allocate time rationally. They analyze the different demands on their time and then decide logically what should be done.

Feeling preference people will experience anxiety when they cannot use their time according to their own values and feelings. They work better when they can put their whole heart into something and create a schedule to accomodate periods of devotion to one particular topic. Anxiety will be greatest when they are in situations where they have to plan according to external rather than internal needs. For example, if they are students and are taking several courses but are interested only in one course, their frustration/anxiety level will be high if they have to limit time in the course they like.

People who prefer Thinking, particularly if they also are Sensors, may easily get bogged down in detail and lose track of long-range priorities. Unless clear rational reasons for deciding time priority decisions are available, a person who prefers Thinking (T) will have trouble choosing how to use his/her time. He/she will experience anxiety if he/she cannot make sense out of the way time is structured. Anxiety also can be generated when two people of opposite preferences try mutually to plan events. The Thinkers want to discuss reasons for allocating specific time resources, while the Feelers want to do what feels right and therefore become frustrated with having to justify their feelings.

Judging (J) Versus Perceiving (P)

People who prefer Judging (J) like organization. In many respects they are good time managers because they like to organize and follow schedules and patterns. They prefer to organize the world around them, while people with the Perceiving (P) preference like to be flexible and respond to the world at any given moment. Schedules and time management often are constricting to Perceivers. They like spontaneity and freedom rather than organization.

Schedules and time management are perhaps the most crucial variables as far as time related anxiety. Persons with a strong preference for Perception will be quite anxious and frustrated if they are forced to follow a rigid schedule. In a sense, to follow a schedule is to deny a part

189

of themselves. On the other hand if a Judger (J) is prevented from arranging and planning time, the individual will have a strong underlying sense of anxiety and feeling that he/she is losing control.

Imagine a marriage between a Perceiver (P) and a Judger (J). Jack, the Judger, comes home and begins to fix dinner. He plans to spend forty-five minutes cooking a meal that has been planned ahead on a weekly menu. His wife, Patty Perceiver, comes home late (she stopped to browse in a bookstore) and says she feels like going out for dinner. Bam, conflict and anxiety! Actually, over the long run, Jack and Patty probably will help each other learn to understand and respect new behaviors and values.

The key to managing time-related anxiety is to be able to develop skills and abilities related to your less preferred function. If you prefer Perception, you probably need to learn how to be organized while still maintaining some flexibility. In nearly every field of endeavor you need some way of organizing time, so try to overcome your resistance to organization and develop a way of scheduling time that is acceptable to you. If you are a Judger and suffer from anxiety when your schedule is interrupted, you need to learn flexibility. Try to develop your ability to be spontaneous. Practice changing your schedule or doing something on the spur of the moment. Learning to deal with life's surprises will help you be less anxious and probably more efficient.

TIME MANAGEMENT SKILLS

Anxiety frequently comes as a result of poor time management skills. When you are not using time effectively, the sense of low productivity and loss of control often creates a general sense of frustration and anxiety. The overemphasis on time and its scarcity identified earlier (Chapter 7) as "hurry sickness" sometimes is related to this inability to manage time effectively. In this instance low productivity and inability to get things done produce a kind of frantic moving from activity to activity with no sense of accomplishment or achievement. In fact the tension and anxiety reduce efficiency so that the person feels he/she has to run faster always glancing at the clock in the background.

In addition to helping you manage time-related anxiety, time management can have profound effects on your success in many aspects of life. If you are a student, effective time management can mean the difference between C and B+ grades. If you are a physician, effective time management will help you improve your practice and quality of care that you provide. If you are a business person, time management will help you more effectively balance and "prioritize" (place in rank order of importance) your work and perhaps lead to faster promotions and more job satisfaction.

You should examine several aspects of time management as possible areas for improvement:

1. goal setting and long-range planning;
2. daily scheduling and prioritizing;
3. procrastination, distraction, and other problems; and
4. balance.

Change and improvement in these areas is related clearly to a number of important life issues. Goal setting is usually part of the value clarification process. Dealing with procrastination, distractions, and similar problems requires examining your general life-style. In a sense, the way you use time represents your approach to life.

Goal Setting and Long-Range Planning

The first step in effectively managing time is to develop an explicit statement of your long-range goals. This statement of goals will allow you to assess periodically your progress and to judge specific activities in relation to your goals. Setting these long-range goals may be more difficult than you imagine. The process can force you to confront decisions that you have been putting off, or value issues that you don't want to handle. The notion of long-term goals scares people because they consider the choices involved as unchangeable. College students, for example, often have great trouble setting career goals because they think the choice locks them into a career for life. Long-range goals are not necessarily forever. They can be changed and modified in all kinds of ways.

If you have trouble setting long-range goals, try to keep yourself from viewing them as permanent. You may only want to set up intermediate goals leaving long-range goal decisions until later. If you have set long-range goals, you also may desire to set intermediate goals related to each long-range goal. Remember also that you need goals in different life areas. In Table 11.4 are examples of long-range and intermediate goals. You can understand that long-range and intermediate goals can provide you with a means of organizing your time, if these goals are truly priorities.

Long-range *planning* involves considering time over a period of months or years and roughing out time frames for your goals. Table 11.4 on the following page is an example of a long-range plan developed by a young woman who first set long-range and then intermediate goals. Next these goals were placed on a timetable related to expected achievement (goal) in terms of age.

Remember that the plan shown in Table 11.4 is not necessarily permanent, but it does give this young woman a rough idea of her goals and her timetable to achieve those goals. She may find that some of the goals are not realistic. Maybe time will not be available for guitar lessons, or maybe she will get interested in something else. Maybe the right man will come along early or maybe he will not come along at all. Life may not be very predictable, but her chances of getting what she wants are increased by planning and goal setting.

This long-range set of goals and plans can be helpful in managing time on a day-to-day basis. The young woman in the example may one day be sitting in her room at college feeling anxious because school work is piling up.

When she looks at her long range goals (which she has written and put over her desk), she realizes that she is spending too much time on activities that just are not a priority for her. By cutting back on these non-priority activities she increases her available time and decreases feelings of pressure and anxiety.

Daily Scheduling and Prioritizing

The heart of effective time management is in day-to-day time organization. Almost everyone needs some kind of system to regulate time, very few people can go through their days doing what they feel like doing from moment to moment. That is perhaps the ideal as far as regulating anxiety, but it does not seem to work in our particular culture.

Scheduling and prioritizing time can be done in a number of ways. The simplest way is perhaps the "list every morning" system. You start out every day by making a list of things that you want to get done that day. Then you decide which are priorities and which you will work on

Table 11.4

Example of a Young Women's Long-Range Goals, Intermediate Goals,
and a Long-Range Plan Related to Chronological Age

LONG-RANGE PLANNING

Long-Range Goals	*Intermediate Goals*
1. Become successful tax attorney	1a. Complete college with 3.5 average
	b. Take a pre-law curriculum
2. Become proficient guitar player	2a. Complete guitar lessons
	b. Practice three hours a week
3. Acquire vacation home in the mountains	3a. Save money to buy land
	b. Visit different locales during vacations
4. Achieve satisfying family life with two children	4a. Meet and date different men
	b. Join interest/recreation groups to meet men
5. Be at ease and successful in social situations	5a. Complete communication skills course
	b. Attend a variety of social functions

LONG-RANGE PLAN
Related to Chronological Age

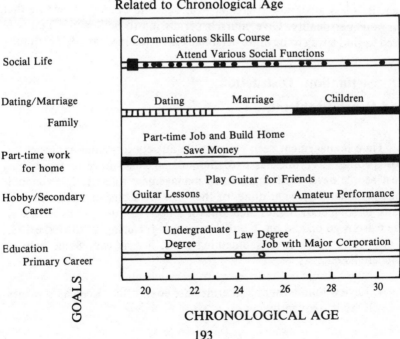

193

when. An understanding of your own best work rhythms and conditions is helpful. If you work best from 9-12 in the morning, then you will want to plan your most difficult work for that time. Or, if you work best in a certain office or location, you will want to arrange a time so that you can take advantage of your preferences. Alan Lakein, who has written a business-oriented book entitled, *How to Control Your Life and Time,* suggests an ABC system for priorities with A's being highest and C's being lowest priority. He suggested trying to eliminate as many C's (low priority items) as possible. And he made the telling point that many people spend too much time on trivia that is not even remotely related to their goals.

Some people find it more helpful to map out a time schedule for a week at a time, assigning specific hours to specific tasks. This type of schedule is likely to appeal to someone who prefers structure and relatively tight control. A major advantage over the "list every day" system is that you plan a week at a time so you can balance out your activities over several days.

If all of this is sounding dreadful to you, it probably means that you are an INFP, Introvert who has trouble keeping track of time, likes to do what feels is most important, and prefers an unstructured approach to the world. If you do feel negative about scheduling, think of the benefits—less anxiety and greater achievement. Create a schedule that fits your personality. Give yourself permission to be flexible. You may need to find a way to be more personally involved in what you are doing.

Procrastination, Distraction, And Other Problems

Time management seems a sensible anxiety lessening approach to most people. Everyone has tried time management once or twice, but most people never really make time management a habit. They cannot quite get what they want done, or they just are a bit unrealistic in their plans, or somebody invites them out for a beer, . . . or . . . or . . . or . . . The reasons go on and on. No real substitute for being motivated exists. If one really wants to get something done, he/she can. Some helpful hints are listed:

1. Review long-term and intermediate goals often. Keep a list where you will see it frequently.

2. Continually try to eliminate unnecessary tasks that you do not enjoy and are not related to your goals.

3. Take advantage of your natural cycles, schedule the most difficult activities when you are the sharpest.

4. Learn how to say "no" to people, including spouses, friends, children, and parents.

5. Reward yourself for effective time management.

6. Solicit cooperation from those around you. Let your spouse, family members, roommate, and others know about your efforts to manage time.

7. Attend to your needs for spontaneity. Do not be inflexible.

8. Do not set yourself up to fail. Be realistic and work toward an individualized approach that makes sense for you.

9. Record things—the process of putting schedules, priorities, etc. on paper is helpful in itself.

Balance

One mistake that individuals frequently make in trying to manage their time comes when they ignore the need for various activities. Everyone needs a time schedule that allows for a balanced life. If a person only has time to work or play, he/she will be anxious because of the imbalance. Allow time for exercise, recreation, adequate sleep, socializing, and other important needs. Even if an individual feels pressed to focus all of his/her attention on one activity, he/she probably will be more efficient and less anxious if he/she attends to his/her needs in all areas. Naturally, the type of balance varies. Some people like to be involved intensely in a particular project however most individuals have a variety of demands put upon them and cannot devote all of their time or energy in such a singular fashion.

No matter how good you are in arranging time, if you do not account for your various needs, you will be less productive and more anxious.

SUMMARY

1. Anxiety is related to one's perceptions and attitudes toward time.

2. The feeling that time is scarce, "hurry sickness," is prevalent in our society and seems to be a major factor in time-related anxiety.

3. Three approaches are helpful in managing time-related anxiety: (a) working toward decreasing Type A behavior, (b) understanding attitudes and personality variables related to perception and use of time, and (c) improving time management skills.

4. Friedman and Rosenman (1973) identified a cluster of attitudes and behaviors, Type A, related to stress and heart disease.

5. Friedman and Rosenman contend that Type A behavior, which is characterized by an aggressive and chronic need to do more and more in less and less time, is the number one cause of heart disease. They label people who do not have this complex of behaviors and attitudes as Type B.

6. A number of strategies can be helpful in decreasing Type A behavior:

   a. Take an honest look at yourself.

   b. Clarify your values.

   c. Don't compete unnecessarily.

   d. Readjust your attitudes toward time.

   e. Create peaceful surroundings for yourself.

   f. Identify and modify specific Type A behaviors.

   g. Explore the meaning of life in new ways.

7. Carl Jung's personality typology can be used to understand the relationship between personality, use and perception of time, and time-related anxiety.

8. The Keirsey Temperament Sorter can be used to assess your preferences on Jung's four basic functions.

9. An understanding of your preferences in each area will help you become more aware of how your use and perception of time can cause excessive anxiety.

10. The Four Jungian preferences are Introversion/Extroversion, Intuition/Sensing, Thinking/Feeling, and Judging/Perceiving.

11. The loss of productivity and personal control that comes from poor time management skills often creates anxiety.

12. The "hurry sickness" mentioned by Friedman and Rosenman (1973) can be a result of frantic attempts to accomplish, resulting, at least partially, from poor time management skills.

13. Effective time management involves: (a) setting goals and priorities; (b) effective daily/weekly scheduling and prioritizing; (c) overcoming procrastination, distractions, and other problems; and (d) achieving a balanced schedule.

14. An explicit statement (in writing) of long-range and intermediate goals provides a reference point for prioritizing daily activities. Keeping these goals in mind also helps counter lagging motivation by helping you connect future goals with present activity.

15. Forgetting about balance in your schedule is easy if you are working toward a specific set of goals. Remember however that everyone has a variety of needs to meet and your general level of efficiency goes down if you do not attend to all of them in some way.

SELF-ASSESSMENT
DISCUSSION QUESTIONS

1. What does time mean to you? Is it scarce?

2. How did your attitudes toward time develop? Do you remember any family attitudes toward time?

3. How would you define Type A Behavior? How do Type A personality individuals view time?

4. Do you agree with Friedman and Rosenman's characterization of Type A and Type B Behavior? Why or why not?

5. Do you identify Type A characteristics in yourself? Do you have any sense of why you behave or feel that way?

6. Would it be difficult for you to change your Type A behavior characteristics? What would it take to make you change?

7. How did you react to the suggestions for changing Type A Behavior? Did any of them seem applicable or not applicable to you?

8. Why is it helpful to set specific life goals? What if you set life goals that require Type A Behavior to achieve?

9. How do Introverts and Extroverts differ in regard to time-related anxiety?

10. How do Intuitors and Sensors differ in regard to time-related anxiety?

11. How do Thinkers and Feelers differ in regard to time-related anxiety?

12. How do Judgers and Perceivers differ in regard to time-related anxiety?

13. Which of the characteristics discussed under the different preferences apply to you?

14. Do you agree with the preferences indicated for you on the Keirsey Temperament Sorter?

15. How would you characterize your current time management methods?

16. Do you have a set of long-range goals? Are they explicitly stated?

17. What is your attitude toward goal setting?

18. What are the advantages to goal setting? Do you see any disadvantages?

19. What kind of daily prioritizing system do you use?

20. Why are people often turned-off to time scheduling? What negative reactions do you have?

21. Can you identify any specific distractions or problems that you have with time management?

22. What is meant by balance with regard to time schedules? How would you rate your own balance?

ACTIVITIES

Activity 11.3 MODIFYING "HURRY SICKNESS"

Purpose: To help you develop a plan to modify your Type A Behavior.

Instructions: Review the suggestions for changing Type A Behavior and list three ways that you can apply each suggestion being as concise as possible. Discuss your ideas with another person in your group or with a friend. Try some of your ideas during the next week and record your reactions. Review your experiences with your discussion partner and revise your ideas as necessary.

Activity 11.4 PERSONALITY PREFERENCES AND ANXIETY

Purpose: To examine personality preference and time-related anxiety.

Instruction: Review your preferences as shown on the Keirsey Temperament Sorter i.e. Extroversion/Introversion, Intuition/Sensing, Thinking/Feeling, and Judging/Perceiving. For each preference, list one potential problem with time-related anxiety and one potential time-related communication problem. Discuss your responses with a person in your work group or with a friend. Try to find a person with some different preferences so that you can compare and contrast perceptions.

Activity 11.5 LONG-RANGE GOALS AND PLANS

Purpose: To develop planning and goal setting interest and skill.

Instruction: Compose a list of your long-range and intermediate goals. Refer to Table 11.3 for examples. Try to include goals from different life areas. After you have listed goals, try to devise a long-range plan similar to the one in Table 11.3. Discuss your list and time plan with a person in your work group or with a friend. Ask the person to help you evaluate your long-range plans by answering the question, "Are they realistic?"

Activity 11.6 TIME ASSESSMENT

Purpose: To assess current time use.

Instructions: Keep a chart of how you spend your time during the next week. Be as detailed as possible. After you have kept this record for about a week, add the hours that you spend in different kinds of activities, i.e. sleeping, eating, working, reading, exercising, watching TV, etc. Analyze the results in light of your expressed goals. Are you spending time on things that are important to you? How much time is wasted or unproductive? Is there any kind of balance? How do you feel about your use of time? Discuss your schedule with someone in your work group or with a friend.

Activity 11.7 TIME MANAGEMENT

Purpose: To encourage experimentation with different time management methods.

Instructions: Experiment with two different ways to prioritize your daily schedule, i.e. daily lists, weekly schedules, time categories for certain activities, etc. After trying each system for a few days, evaluate your reactions. Does one system seem to work better, feel more comfortable, have more pitfalls, or depend too much on other people? From what you learn from this experiment develop a system that works for you and use it for the next week. Modify it until you devise a method that works.

BIBLIOGRAPHY

Friedman, M., & Rosenman, R. H. *Type A behavior and your heart*. New York: Alfred A. Knopf, 1974.

Jung, C. *Psychological types*. New York: Harcourt Brace, 1923.

Keirsey, D., & Bates, M. *Please understand me: An essay on temperament styles*. Del Mar, California: Promethean Books, Inc., 1978.

Lakein, A. *How to get control of your time and your life*. New York: David McKay Co., 1973.

Myers, I. *The Myers-Briggs type indicator*. Palo Alto, California: Consulting Psychologist Press, 1977.

Myers, I. *The Myers-Briggs type indicator*. Princeton, New Jersey: Educational Testing Service, 1962.

Nowotny, H. Time structuring and time measurement: On the interrelation between timekeepers and social time. In J. T. Fraser, & N. Lawrence (Eds.). *The Study of Time II: Second Conference of the International Society for the Study of Time. New York: Springer-Verlag, 1975.*

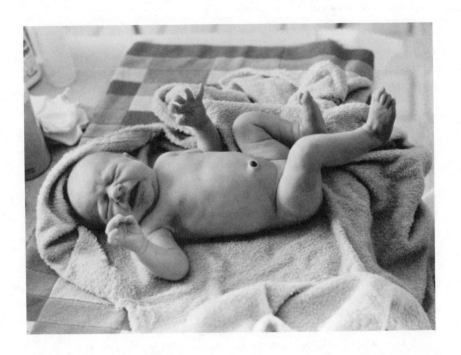

A new baby creates many anxiety management challenges for parents.

Chapter 12

LIFE TRANSITIONS

In one way or another we all struggle with life transitions. Change is an inevitable part of life and the accompanying anxiety also affects us all. The process of growing older is in itself anxiety producing. A child's perception of the world and society's expectations of him/her change as he/she gets older. A teenager views and experiences life quite differently than someone in their forty's. Although this kind of change is a part of normal growth and development, it still moves the individual into uncharted waters. Anxiety is no less real because it is normal; and if not managed effectively, it can become a problem.

Anxiety is also a part of changes and transitions that are not developmental. These changes occur throughout life, often without warning. Examples would be the death of a loved one, discovery of a life-threatening illness, loss of a job, or change in family status (marriage, divorce). Many of the events and circumstances, for example growing old, that precipitate change seem beyond a person's control—things happen and the individual somehow has to accomodate him/herself to these changes. The secret of managing anxiety related to these changes is to focus on the power that you do have to control how you *react* to change.

203

LIFE DEVELOPMENT

Current popular psychology literature includes many articles about adult development. Hearing people talk about their "mid-life" crisis or about their husband, wife, or friend going through "a stage" is common. This comment formerly applied only to children. Society is becoming aware of the fact that people grow and change throughout their lifetime. This awareness is helpful because it encourages people to consider the patterns and forces at work in their lives.

An understanding of how development generally occurs can help you better accept and understand life changes and transitions. If you know that the late thirties and early forties are characterized by a general self-questioning and acceptance of life's limitations, you will be better able to cope with these feelings in your own life. This understanding will help you manage anxiety and also free you to accept and enjoy the progress of your life.

Many different theories attempt to explain how a person develops. Erik Erikson (1950) conceptualized development as a series of stages that are partly a result of biological maturation and partly a result of social roles and expectations. His theory was the first to include the entire life span. Although he characterized himself as a psychoanalyst and claimed a Freudian orientation, he departed considerably from Freud's emphasis on early psychosexual childhood stages. Erikson also first introduced and discussed the concept of identity and how it conforms to a developmental framework.

He identified eight stages of man with each stage characterized by a central conflict between two poles of the developmental issue that is dominant in that stage. The struggle and a kind of balance are necessary parts of development. The first four stages of his theory occur between birth and about twelve years of age, beginning adolescence. Although the conflicts in these first four stages sometimes are repeated, they never come into the same type of focus in adolescence or adulthood. The last four stages, five through eight, are the most helpful in understanding anxiety related to adult development. Following is a brief outline of each of these adolescent and adult stages.

Identity Versus Role Diffusion

In Stage Five which begins with adolescence the period of childhood ends and the struggle for adulthood becomes the central focus. Erikson characterizes the conflict as a struggle between identity versus role diffusion. The growth of sexual organs and related feelings and changing social expectations are significant influences during this period. In the sometimes desperate search for identity, young people often overidentify with specific heroes, causes, or ideologies. At times, as a way of fighting confusion, groups and cliques that adolescents form can be quite illusive and cruel. A kind of selfless infatuation with another person also is common.

Understanding what Erikson means by identity is somewhat easier if one subdivides identity into several spheres. An individual must develop an identity in several different spheres. A person must have an occupational identity, a sexual identity, a social identity, and an ethical or moral identity. The demand for growth and integration in all these areas, set against a society that constantly is defining new roles, makes the achievement of identity a formidable task in modern society. Coupled with these identity conflicts are the needs adolescents have for idealism and perfection. The high rate of adolescent suicide is probably the result of acute identity confusion.

Intimacy Versus Isolation

In Stage Six the young adult moves from concern with identity, an inward focus, to a search for intimacy and sharing, an external focus. Note the importance of the crucial relationship of one stage to another. If a young person has not developed some sense of identity, he/she probably will not be able to move on to Stage Six, where a sense of identity is a necessary precursor for the development of intimacy. This period, late teens and early twenties, is when the young person in our culture traditionally chooses a mate.

The conflict between intimacy and isolation is concerned with the question of whether the young person can move beyond involvement with him/herself to involvement with others. This involvement is risky and takes a certain amount of ego strength which can come only as a result of generally successful navigation of the earlier stages. It is particularly a result of a successful formation of the sense of identity. Negative consequences of this stage doom the unsuccessful individual to a life of isolation and inability to share with others on a meaningful level. Although not as serious as the consequences of failure at earlier stages, the isolation is painful and robs life of much of its meaning.

Generativity Versus Stagnation

As in Stages Five and Six, Erikson goes beyond Freud's original psychosexual stages to hypothesize an adult developmental stage with a central conflict between generativity and stagnation, Stage Seven. "I use the word generativity because I mean anything that is generated from generation to generation: children, products, ideas, and works of art." (Evans, 1967, p.51) The conflict essentially concerns an adult developing ways to create and contribute something to the next generation. Whether the rearing of a child or the production of a work of art, the process, according to Erikson, is imbued with a kind of sexual energy. This stage, generativity versus stagnation, and the previous stage, intimacy versus isolation, both involve a movement away from self toward others. The movement is first toward individuals and then toward society. Lack of success in developing a sense of generativity does not lead to psychosis or an inability to live satisfactorily; however, it does prevent a person from achieving full satisfaction from life.

Integrity Versus Despair

In the last Erikson stage, which encompasses old age, the central conflict is between integrity and despair. Integrity, as Erikson defines it, is an ego strength that comes from a successful passage through the previous seven life stages. The absence of integrity results in the despairing of one's life. The difference between an aged person who is at ease with him/herself in his/her life contrasts sharply with the individual who is bitter and constantly bemoaning the way his/her life has gone. This despair and failure to accept one's life make it impossible to face death with wisdom and equanimity.

ANXIETY AND DEVELOPMENT

The conflict inherent in each stage of development can create considerable anxiety. The search for identity in Stage Five is at the base of what for many adolescents is a tumultous time. Anxiety is very difficult for adolescents to manage because of the intensity of feelings. Anxieties experienced in this stage are often a result of interactions between adolescents and their parents. To manage their anxieties, parents and adolescents have to develop effective communication channels. Adolescents need to be able to explore different roles and consider many different aspects of identity. In later adolescence part of identity formulation involves a breaking away from parents.

Arthur Chickering (1964) included the following three steps in this process of developing independence:

1. Emotional autonomy—less emotional reliance on parents;

2. Instrumental independence—being able to try new things, to travel, or to live in new locations; and finally,

3. Interpendence—realization that they live in a social context and that they are dependent in some ways on each other by definition.

Sexual anxieties are prominent during this period. Part of any person's identity is his/her sexual identity. Because of the incredible pressure put on young people by our sexual attitudes which are both repressive and exploitive, the potential for conflict and anxiety is great. Communication and information are the best ways to manage anxiety in this context. If you are an adolescent and you need help, seek out a friend, counselor, or parent. Choose someone you can trust and with whom you can talk over your concerns. If you are a parent, do the same. If you are not comfortable providing information to your adolescent children, work out some alternative way to get them information.

Selecting a career can be enormously anxiety producing. During one's late teens and early twenties pressure begins to build on young men and women to decide their life's career. This process is even more difficult for women because they often are caught between traditional and modern role expectations. Two general ways to manage this kind of anxiety are helpful: (1) actively work toward career decisions, and (2) allow the necessary time for choice even if it requires resisting societal pressures. With the general economic conditions and emphasis on careerism, many young people are being pushed into premature career decisions. This kind of premature choice frequently leads to much anxiety related to career dissatisfaction.

Stage Six, which is characterized by the conflict between intimacy and isolation, is often a time of fear and worry about how to develop intimate relationships. The anxiety related to this fear often is heightened by pressures to choose a mate before one gets too old. Some people do not develop intimate relationships because of these fears and anxieties. Anxiety can be managed best by allowing oneself the time and space necessary to learn how to be intimate and by identifying specific intimacy blocks and problems. An active confrontation of intimacy problems and a resolution to work toward their solution can help overcome anxiety. Participation in group or individual counseling can be helpful.

In the generativity versus stagnation stage, Stage Seven, "late twenties to mid-fifties," anxiety tends to be less focused except at certain crisis points. During this period men and women are confronted with values their lives exhibit and with the increasing finality of their choices. Levinson, in his book, *The Seasons of a Man's Life* (1978), presented a theory of adult male development focusing mostly on the generativity stage. He identifies two transition periods that often induce some kind of identity or general life crisis. The first transition period is the age thirty transition. At about this age the men he studied all went through a period of reappraisal that in many cases led to life changes. He hypothesizes another major transition at around age forty that he called the mid-life transition. During this period another reappraisal takes place. This reappraisal includes a process that he calls "deillusionment," giving up and/or freeing oneself of many youthful illusions and fantasies. A man begins to accept his career limitations and to modify some of his life expectations. These transitions are not necessarily quick, they take from four to five years, and they happen differently for different men. Levinson's theory was developed from his study of a small group of men so that the applicability to women has not been demonstrated. Anxiety is experienced frequently during these transition periods. According to Levinson (1978) sixty-two percent of the men studied experienced a moderate or severe crisis during the age thirty transition and about eight percent during the mid-life transition.

In managing the anxiety related to these transitions, *accepting* and *experiencing* emotional and intellectual turmoil are necessary. The individual needs to use the anxiety creatively rather than to defend against it and the accompanying change. If you are going through one of these periods, you may have special needs to travel, explore by yourself, change family patterns, and so forth. In a sense the best way to manage anxiety is to provide yourself with the freedom or permission to explore new aspects of yourself.

Erikson's last stage, which involves the conflict between ego identity versus despair, centers around looking back over one's life. The anxiety related to this conflict is perhaps less intense than the other steps. Anxiety often comes from fear of death and of growing old. Medical problems, retirement, changed relationships with families, loss of spouse, and fear of being a burden on others can all create anxiety. The challenge is to grow old gracefully and embrace life while one is preparing to let it go. Relationships with young people and with children can help one be aware of the ever renewing cycle of life. Religious beliefs and activities can be comforting as well as meaningful contact with others in the same life stage. Acceptance and awareness that children and grandchildren must experience the vagaries of life themselves can prevent family conflicts. Realistic planning, commitments about medical problems, and plans for death can help decrease anxiety. Activity is imperative in this stage also. Creative use of retirement time can make a great difference.

MAJOR LIFE EVENTS

In addition to transitions and changes that are a part of the regular developmental cycle a number of events such as death, divorce, and pregnancy frequently are accompanied by anxiety. Because anxiety is common in these situations, studying human reactions and coping mechanisms from the perspective of the events is possible. The danger of this approach is in the generalizations that may be made and in the focus on events rather than process. Generalizing is a problem because of the great differences in how people respond to different events. Divorce for one person may be an agonizing event that takes years from which to recover, while for someone else it may be a liberating experience that greatly enhances life.

The most widely known attempt to generalize about anxiety and various life events is Holmes and Rahe's (1967) Social Readjustment Scale. In this scale they listed forty-three life events, from divorce to vacation, that potentially are stress producing. Each event is assigned a value that indicates its relative strength as a stressful event. The scale was developed to study the relationship between the stress associated with these events and susceptibility to illness. In general the higher one's total score the greater the susceptibility to illness during the next year or two. A copy of the scale is included as Table 12.1.

As you read the scale, you may be surprised by the variety of items and by the inclusion of things like "vacation" or "Christmas." Keep in mind that this list is an attempt to generalize about situations that most frequently cause stress. Each item is not necessarily stress producing for all individuals. Several themes seem to be present for the highest scored events. These themes which include death, divorce/separation, career loss/change, and family addition/change, can all be examined from the perspective of anxiety management.

209

Table 12.1

Social Readjustment Scale*

The following scale was developed by Holmes and Rahe (1967) to help investigate the relationship between social readjustment, stress, and susceptibility to illness. They found that a person with a score of 150 during a one year period had a 50-50 chance of developing an illness or health change. With a score of 300 or more a persons chances increased to 90%.

Event	Value	Event	Value
Death of spouse	100	Son or daughter leaving home	29
Divorce	73	Trouble with in-laws	29
Marital separation	65	Outstanding personal achieve-	
Jail term	63	ment	28
Death of close family member	63	Spouse begins or stops work	26
Personal injury or illness	53	Starting or finishing school	26
Marriage	50	Change in living conditions	25
Fired from work	47	Revision of personal habits	24
Marital reconciliation	45	Trouble with boss	23
Retirement	45	Change in work hours, condi-	
Change in family member's		tions	20
health	44	Change in residence	20
Pregnancy	40	Change in schools	20
Sex difficulties	39	Change in recreational habits	19
Addition to family	39	Change in church activities	19
Business readjustment	39	Change in social activities	18
Change in financial status	38	Mortgage or loan under	
Death of close friend	37	$10,000	17
Change to different line of		Change in sleeping habits	16
work	36	Change in number of family	
Change in number of marital		gatherings	15
arguments	35	Change in eating habits	15
Mortgage or loan over		Vacation	13
$10,000	31	Christmas season	12
Foreclosure of mortgage or		Minor violation of the law	11
loan	30		
Change in work responsi-			
bilities	29		

*T.H. Holmes and R.H. Rahe. The social adjustment rating scale. *Journal of Psychosomatic Research, II,* 1967, 213-18.

MANAGING ANXIETY

By this time you have an arsenal of weapons to use in managing anxiety. These different techniques are valuable when you are confronted with some kind of major life change. Your management of physical tension can greatly affect your general ability to cope with the event. If you are recently divorced, for example, and your emotions make you feel as if you are on a roller coaster, practicing some form of regular relaxation is in your best interest. You need every bit of mental clarity and every ounce of energy you can muster to put your life back together. The way you think about the event also can influence the course of your anxiety. If you have just lost your job, you may be inclined to catastrophize and become negative with yourself. At this point you need more than ever to practice being rational and maintaining your perspective.

Several principles can be used to summarize general coping and anxiety management strategies for major life changes:

1. Accept and experience your feelings.

2. Seek out help and support from family and friends.

3. Seek out professional or peer group help.

4. Emphasize physical and nutritional health.

5. Be patient and allow yourself time to recover.

6. Identify and revise short and long-term goals.

7. Plan and experiment with new life patterns and behaviors.

Accept and Experience Your Feelings

People often have a very difficult time allowing themselves to feel. Sometimes potential feelings are so hurtful that individuals attempt to protect themselves by covering up the feelings in some way. This defense sometimes is necessary for a limited period of time; however, it interferes with coping mechanisms if maintained for a prolonged period. Take for example the case of a man recently separated from his wife. His feelings of anger and desperation may be too difficult to deal with at first. He may feel that if he allows himself really to experience his feelings, he will

211

not be able to keep going. After a few weeks he continues to deny these feelings and frequently feels very tense and anxious. In this case the anxiety probably is related to his inability to experience his feelings.

In our society few individuals, particularly men, learn much about how to express and experience feelings. More frequently one learns that controlling his/her feelings and not showing them is desirable. Sometimes control is necessary, but losing the ability to express and experience feelings can be detrimental.

No feelings are more difficult to deal with than those concerning death. Elizabeth Kubler-Ross (1975) has identified the way feelings often are experienced by people who are dying. She identified a five-step process which includes the following stages:

1. Denial: "No, not me."

2. Rage and Anger: "Why me?"

3. Bargaining: "Yes me, but ..."

4. Depression: "Yes, me."

5. Acceptance: "My time is very close now and it is all right."

A kind of chronic anxiety can occur if you do not effectively deal with your emotional reactions to major life changes. The pain of this anxiety may seem less than the pain of hurt or anger but it probably is more insidious. This pain eats away at you and prevents adequate coping.

Seek Out Help and Support
From Family and Friends

Support is absolutely essential in coping with difficult life changes and crises. You need to feel the security of someone who cares and who is available when you need reassurance. The support of family members or other loved ones often is necessary to provide the security necessary to be able to experience powerful negative and frightening emotions. Also you need others to help you keep the event in perspective. What they say to you is not as important as the fact that they are present for you and willing to try to share some of your fear or pain.

Asking for help and support from others is sometimes difficult even if they are very close friends or relatives. The belief that others cannot really understand how you are feeling may be true, but remember that the other person does not have to know exactly how you are feeling. Everyone has experienced loss, pain, and so forth in some way and they will empathize from their own experiences.

You also may feel that asking for support is an unnecessary burden on someone else. Certainly you are asking for time and attention but the other person does have the choice to refuse if he/she cannot spend the time. The prior nature of the relationship is important. If you are close to someone, the chances are good that you have provided them with a sympathetic ear, or better an empathic one, a time or two. If you are resisting the need to seek support from others, try to overcome your reluctance. In the long run you will avoid unnecessary anxiety and work through your transition difficulties much more quickly.

Seek Out Professional or Peer Group Help

Sometimes support from family members and friends is not enough. Generally if you find yourself unable to resume your life within a reasonable time or if the intensity of your reaction is more than friends can handle, you should seek out professional help or a group of people who have undergone similar experiences. If you are changing careers, it may make sense to see a professional counselor or agency that specializes in career change. Or if you have lost a child and find that you just cannot get over the loss, you may want to seek self-help groups of parents in similar situations in your community. Groups for people undergoing all kinds of life transitions have begun recently. The general principle in all these groups is that a kind of sharing, understanding, and advice giving from others in similar situations is very beneficial.

Emphasize Physical and Nutritional Health

Worrying about what you eat or how you exercise when some major crisis has just occured may seem silly, however, this is the point where you really need to deal with stress as effectively as you can. Letting everything including exercise and nutrition slide during periods of anxiety or crisis is common, but just a little effort in these areas can make a big difference. Exercise, in particular, can be very calming and the regularity and intensity of exercise can give you a physical and mental boost.

Be Patient and Give Yourself Time to Recover

Life changes like death, divorce/separation, career loss/change, or family additions/changes have profound effects. They produce anxious, often tumultuous times, and it takes *time* to recover and go on with life. Allow yourself that time. Do not give up hope and feel that things will never get better. You need people around you who will tell you this. In fact, that is a major function of anyone in a support role. Try to allow yourself a period of transition.

Identify and Revise Goals

Even after the most severe life crisis imaginable you eventually have to get back to living your own life. Many life changes require new goals and life patterns. If you have been planning to move to Florida when you retire and your wife or husband dies six months before retirement, your retirement plans and goals need rethinking. A previous plan may no longer be in your best interest. Or if you are happily living as a housewife and mother and suddenly your husband decides that he no longer wants to be married to you, you obviously would have to rethink your future goals and plans.

Don't make any definitive changes in goals immediately after a life crisis. Give yourself time to recover and to get accustomed to your new situation. You may even need a transition year or two before you can begin to reassess some of the long-term goals that you have always held.

Plan and Experiment with New Life Patterns and Behaviors

Everyone has advice on how to cope with difficult life events. Widows are told to get out and meet new men, divorced men are advised to start new hobbies, and parents with a new baby are told not to let the baby come between them. All of these suggestions are perhaps good advice, but they need to come at the right time. Each individual needs to decide when that right time is for him/her. Use an experimental approach. You may have to try several new patterns and behaviors before you find something that feels right.

SUMMARY

1. Life changes and transitions as a result of normal growth and development can cause anxiety because of different roles and situations created.

2. Abrupt life changes and those that radically alter your life style (death, divorce) usually require major life adjustments and frequently produce feelings of anxiety and tension.

3. Erikson's (1950) theory of developmental life stages is particularly helpful in understanding the conflicts and anxieties related to normal growth and development.

4. In Stage Five which covers ages 12-18 (adolescence), the major conflict is between identity and role confusion. During this period young people are searching for an identity in a number of areas including: sexual, career, social, and ethical.

5. In this stage, adolescents should have the freedom to explore different aspects of identity and ultimately to begin to move away from dependence on parents. Young people at this stage need support with freedom. Many anxieties come as a result of conflicts between parents and adolescents and this kind of anxiety is managed best through communication and understanding from both parties.

6. In Stage Six which occurs in the late teens and early twenties, the dominant conflict is between intimacy and isolation. During this period the young adult moves from a kind of internal focus on identity to a more external focus on developing the ability to be intimate.

7. Stage Seven covers a very large segment of the life span, from the mid-twenties to old age. Erikson called the major conflict "generativity versus stagnation." In essence this is the period of life when the focus is on productivity and contribution to society.

8. In Stage Eight the conflict is between integrity and despair. The person at this stage struggles between feeling despair for what he/she has missed in life and satisfaction for what he/she has experienced.

9. Because of conflicts in each of these stages, individuals often experience varying degrees of anxiety in each stage. Identifying and understanding the issues surrounding these conflicts can help in managing anxiety.

10. Anxieties related to the intimacy versus isolation stage are most often a result of fear and inability to allow intimacy to develop. Sometimes professional help is necessary to overcome intimacy blocks.

11. Although mid-life crises have been popularized to the point of becoming passe, they are still very common. Levinson (1978) recognizes two general crisis points, one at around thirty and another around forty. A period of reassessment and freedom to consider life style changes can help with anxiety related to these crises.

12. Major life events cause stress. Holmes and Rahe (1967) listed these life events in their Social Readjustment Scale.

13. Events that appear to cause the most stress for the most people are death, divorce/separation, career loss/change, and family addition/change.

14. The following principles outline an effective approach to managing anxiety related to stressful life events and changes:

    a. Accept and experience your feelings.

    b. Seek out help and support from family and friends.

    c. Seek out professional or peer group help.

    d. Emphasize physical and nutritional health.

    e. Be patient and allow yourself time to recover.

    f. Identify and revise short and long-term goals.

    g. Plan and experiment with new life patterns and behaviors.

SELF-ASSESSMENT
DISCUSSION QUESTIONS

1. How can the normal process of growing up create anxiety?

2. Name two or three aspects of your own development that seemed to cause anxiety? Why was the anxiety generated?

3. What is meant by identity versus role diffusion?

4. Can you describe how you developed your own sense of identity? Was anxiety involved? How?

5. What are some of the conflicts related to identity that teenagers experience?

6. Why are anxieties in the adolescent stage often related to interactions between parents and adolescents?

7. Why is sexual identity a particularly anxiety arousing issue?

8. What were the two or three strongest anxieties for you as a teenager?

9. What is the danger of someone's inability to manage anxiety during the adolescent stage?

10. What is meant by intimacy versus isolation?

11. Why is it so frightening to be intimate with others?

12. How would you describe your own reaction to intimacy?

13. Does intimacy imply sexual relations?

14. Is it easier for women to be intimate?

15. Do you need certain skills to be intimate?

16. What is meant by generativity versus stagnation?

17. What are some of the ways that people in the generativity stage feel productive?

18. What is meant by mid-life crisis?

19. Why does the feeling of being nonproductive often cause anxiety?

20. Do you agree with the Holmes and Rahe scale? Can you name other important stressful life events?

21. Why is accepting and experiencing your feelings important?

22. How do you handle your feelings during a stressful life event?

23. Is seeking out help from friends and family members easy for you?

217

24. When is professional consultation advisable to help someone manage anxiety from a major life event?

25. What kind of stressful life events would require a transition period?

ACTIVITIES

Activity 12.1 ANXIETY AND DEVELOPMENTAL STAGES

Purpose: To examine anxiety related to life stages.

Instructions: Identify your own stage of development according to Erikson's theory. Does the central conflict seem to apply to you? List other conflicts and anxieties that seem related to your own life stage. List your current methods for managing anxiety and others that you would like to use. Discuss these questions and your answers with a partner or in a small group.

Activity 12.2 ANXIETY AND INTIMACY

Purpose: To explore anxieties related to intimacy.

Instructions: Describe one or two intimate relationships that you have experienced and list two or three aspects of each relationship that created anxiety. How did you cope with these? Discuss with a partner or in a small group.

Activity 12.3 LIFE EVENTS

Purpose: To examine the relationship between life events and anxiety.

Instructions: Complete the Social Readjustment Scale (Table 12.1) by adding points for the number of events that you have experienced during the last year. The meaning of your score is outlined in the first paragraph of the scale.

Activity 12.4 COPING WITH ANXIETY RELATED TO LIFE EVENTS

Purpose: To identify personal anxiety management strategies.

Instructions: Choose one event in your life that has been most stressful for you. Answer the following questions:

1. What feelings did you experience?

2. Did you accept and experience your feelings immediately? How long did it take for you to accept and experience your feelings?

3. Did you ask anyone for help or support? Was it easy or difficult to ask for help or support? Was it helpful?

4. How did you react physically to the stress?

5. Did you allow yourself time to recover?

6. Did you develop any new life goals or patterns?

7. What did you find most helpful in coping with your anxiety?

BIBLIOGRAPHY

Chickering, A. W. *Education and identity.* San Francisco: Jossey Bass, 1969.

Erikson, E. H. *Childhood and society.* New York: Norton, 1950.

Evans, R. *Dialogue with Erik Erikson.* New York: Harper and Row, 1967.

Holmes, T. H., & Rahe, R. H. The social readjustment scale. *Journal of Psychsomatic Research II,* 1967, pp. 213-218.

Kubler, R. E. *Death: The final stage of growth.* Englewood Cliffs, New Jersey: Prentice-Hall, 1975.

Levinson, D. J. *The seasons of a man's life.* New York: Ballantine Books, 1978.

INDEX

INDEX

INDEX

224

226

P

Pelletier, K R 10, 13, 16, 25, 43, 44, 45, 51, 53, 70, 71, 76, 89

Perception, time 18-9

Perry, W 167

Personality
extroversion 186-7
introversion 186-7

Physical tension techniques
exercises 17
nutrition 17
relaxation 17

A Physician's Handbook on Orthomolecular Medicine, 89

Please Understand Me: An Essay on Temperment Styles 185, 201

Pollack, M L 80-1, 82, 89

Positive Addiction 89

Powell, J 150

Practice of Behavior Therapy, The 13, 67, 150

Preferences
feeling 188-9
intuition 187-8
judging 189-90
perceiving 189-90
sensing 187-8
thinking 188-9

Progressive deep muscle relaxation
deep muscle relaxation 60

Progressive Relaxation 67

Psychological Types 201

Psychology Today 48, 53

Psychosomatics 13

R

Rahe, R H 7, 13, 210, 216, 219

Rational beliefs
practicing 105

Rational Emotive Psychotherapy 18

Reason and Emotion in Psychotherapy 25, 110, 126

Relaxation
self-statements 121-2
cueing 47-8

Relaxation Response, The 5, 3, 25, 44, 53

Richardson, F 61, 67

Rogers, C 150, 153, 167

Rodale, J I 89

Rokeach, M 154, 167

Rosenman, R H 18, 25, 169, 170, 171, 174, 176, 201

Royal Canadian Air Force Exercise Plans for Physical Fitness 89

S

Sarason, I G 13

Science of Breath 67

Scientific Research on Transcendental Meditation 46, 53

Seasons of a Man's Life, The 208, 219

Self-statements
coping 121-2
negative 95
positive 114-121, 122
reaction stage 116-8, 118-9, 120-1
rehearsing 121-2
reinforcing 120-1
relaxation 117-8, 121-2
stress, coping 114-21

Simon, S B 156, 167

Social interaction skills
group situations 134-5
listening 132-3
self-disclose 135
small talk 133-4

229

ABOUT
THE
AUTHOR

James Archer, Jr., Ph.D.
Licensed Psychologist

ABOUT THE AUTHOR

James Archer, Jr., Ph.D., is Director of University Counseling Center, University of Florida in Gainesville, Florida. Previously after completing his Ph.D. at Michigan State University, his position was Associate Director at the Center for Counseling, University of Delaware, Newark, Delaware. Also, he assisted in the administration of a comprehensive university counseling and psychological service center.

Having taught and supervised in several areas, Dr. Archer's work included anxiety management, assertion training, time management, crisis intervention, communication skills, study skills, sex roles, racial awareness, and helping relationships. He also has taught graduate courses in counseling theory, college student development, group counseling, and practicum and has served as a clinical supervisor of graduate students, interns, and staff psychologists.

From 1978-1979, he was President of the Delaware Psychological Association. He is active in the American Psychological Association, American Personnel and Guidance Association, American College Personnel Association, Association for Specialists in Group Work, and Phi Kappa Phi. Dr. Archer also has maintained a part-time private practice. He has been involved in several organizations as a consultant and has conducted various workshops.

Dr. Archer has authored articles in several journals: *Counseling Psychology, College Student Personnel, Personnel and Guidance*, and has served on the Editorial Board for the *Journal for Specialists in Group Work*.

232